Return to Father

Archetypal Dimensions of the Patriarch

Gregory Max Vogt

Spring Publications, Inc.
Dallas, Texas

This book is dedicated to Russell Lockhart, "don Russ,"
with gratitude for his encouragement to be a buffalo rather
than a cow, to head right into the storm.

Spring Publications, Inc.; P.O. Box 222069; Dallas, Texas 75222

© 1991 by Spring Publications, Inc. All rights reserved. First printing 1991
in the United States of America. Text printed on acidfree paper Cover
designed and produced by Margot McLean. Cover painting by Jared
Fitzgerald, *A Man in the City,* guache, 8½ X 9¼. Interior art from *Old-
Fashioned Frames and Borders,* ed. Carol Belanger Grafton (Dover)

Library of Congress Cataloging-in-Publication Data
Vogt, Gregory Max.
    Return to father : archetypal dimensions of the patriarch /
Gregory Max Vogt.
      p.   cm.
    Includes bibliographical references.
    ISBN 0-88214-347-6
    1. Patriarchy. 2. Fathers. 3. Archetype (Psychology) 4. Men—
—Psychology. I. Title.
GN479.6.V64 1991
306.85'8—dc20   91-19850
                                          CIP

Contents

Acknowledgments   v

Author's Note   vi

Part I: Exile and Return
   Introduction   3
   Men's House   19
   The Patriarch: Images from Various Writers   29

Part II: dh-mo
   The Father Is the House: Excursions on
   Language, the Images of Pattern and Repair,
   and the Archetypal Father Warrior   45
     Repair   51
     Father Warrior   64
     The Female Patriarch   79

Part III: Three Male Bodies
   The Hunter's Body   85
     Cruelty   89
     The Hunter's Edge and Consciousness   90
     Suffering   95
     Predation   96
     Preparation for Death   97

Contents

Penetration and Penetrativeness	101
The Scrotum and the Hunter's Game Bag	104
Scrotum and Belly	106
The Hand That Embraces the Weapon	106
Scarcity of Game	108
The Body of the Builder	113
The Concreteness of the Vegetative Body	118
The Builder's Body and the Tree	119
The Builder's Sacrificial Body	124
The Unified Body	125
Containers, Vessels, Belly, Scrotum	127
Assemblage and Body Parts, Male Healing, Repair	128
The Builder's Place	130
The Philosopher's Body	147
The Philosopher's *Pater*	147
Lust and Water	151
Sexual Battle	157
The Philosopher in His Village	161
Return to Father	163
Works Cited	164
Related Readings	167

Acknowledgments

"Axe Handles," excerpted from *Axe Handles*, copyright © 1983 by Gary Snyder. Published by North Point Press and reprinted by permission.

"The Salmon Leap," from *The Complete Poems of Hugh MacDiarmid, Volume I*, copyright © 1978 Christopher Murray Grieve, 1985 Valda Grieve. Published by Martin, Brian & O'Keeffe and reprinted by permission.

"My Father's Wedding 1924," from *The Man in the Black Coat Turns* by Robert Bly, copyright © 1981 by Robert Bly. Used by permission of Doubleday, a division of Bantam Doubleday Dell Publishing Group, Inc.

Excerpts from "Meditations," by René Descartes. Reprinted by permission of Macmillan Publishing Company from *Discourse on Method and Meditations*, translated by Laurence J. Lafleur. Copyright © 1960 by Macmillan Publishing Company.

Excerpt from *Meetings with Remarkable Men* by G. I. Gurdjieff, copyright © E. P. Dutton and Company. Used by permission of E. P. Dutton and Company.

Author's Note

Any and all anthropological statements made in this book are to be read as fable and metaphor, a protein for the hungry male soul. The author makes no claim to be anthropology scholar, mythographer or mythologist. He might rather hope to be known as heir to Telemachos, himself heir and son to Odysseus—patriarch, king, roamer of the strange world, teller of tales.

Part I: Exile and Return

Introduction

Father being the loneliest word in the one
language and a word only . . .

John Berryman

It's a wise child that knows its own father.

Homer

1.

Most men alive today remember a time, not long gone,
when the word "patriarch" and the word "masculine" were
used as terms of distinction and were reserved as particularly
dignified terms for certain outstanding contributors to their
time. Fatherhood was a well-defined, noble endeavor, and
the highest and noblest goal of fatherhood was to be a
patriarch.

A patriarch was not only a father of the family but also
someone considerably more elevated: the father of a spiritual
tradition, such as Abraham, Isaac or Jacob; someone of
supreme importance in history or literature; a dignitary; a
person regarded as a founder, such as a founder of a town,
an order, an organization, an institution, school of thought;
or, in local usage, a venerable old man, a veteran, someone
who embodied the past and its meaning, the oldest living
representative of a profession or an art.

Old age carried a dignity of power and achievement, endurance and memory, something gradually gained in the tissue of a man through years of endeavor. A young man dreamed of achievement, of power, endurance, competition, the exercise of prowess, the practice of masculine virtues that would, over time, build in him the satisfaction of memory, recognition and honor that the patriarch represented.

Fatherhood in the family denoted merit, power, status and even a kind of righteousness. Fatherhood to the culture remained an even loftier goal ripe with potential rewards, not the least of which was the connection with the continuity of history.

One might become a patriarch.

This vision was shattered, or at least visibly shaken, by a fundamental, pervasive and consummately developed challenge from what is now called the women's movement. A staggering volume of literature has exposed the dark underbelly of patriarchy—that the ascent of the patriarch has been at the cost of the subordination and exploitation of women.

For example, Gerda Lerner proposes that, over a twenty-six hundred year span, men gradually increased control over women until women were seen to be subordinate creatures from the physical to the spiritual domains. The primary method, according to her, has been control of women's sexuality, which then expanded to all areas of experience, the economic, political and social, etc. The evidence Lerner has amassed is impressive in scope. She draws material from archeology, anthropology, religious studies, myth studies and historical documents of all kinds (such as the code of Hammurabi, which is roundly scourged for its denigrating policies toward women).

The often ruthless exploitation of women by men is well-

documented by now. The evidence is far too extensive to require citation here. An identified evil in our society is
patriarchy or the patriarchal system, with its components of
competition, superiority, hierarchies, boastfulness, challenge,
the call to victory, conquest and power, intellectual self-
assuredness, heroism and consciousness.

The evidence is clear and irrefutable that a particular
kind of patriarchy is responsible for an attitude and action
of cruel exploitation of others, particularly of women and
children. However, to define patriarchy so narrowly misses
the richness of the figure and condemns the thinker to the
same kind of one-up, one-down thinking that he or she is
repudiating in him. In other words, if one begins to think
that patriarchy is a "worthless perspective" and denies this
archetype, one is practicing the same kind of subordination
and exploitation that one is castigating.

Certainly, it must not have been the intent of the writers
and thinkers within the women's movement to denigrate men
who have achieved, or to attack the concept of nobility in
fatherhood, or to scorn or humiliate men because of their
male tissue. And yet the male psyche and body limp fatherless
through the modern landscape, alien and confused, history-
less and impoverished.

Our old men are seen as fools and clowns, barracked
in the nursing homes or shuffling like zombies in the shopping malls. Can one imagine Donald Trump asking an old
grandfather of the Hopis for wisdom? What could be sillier
than old rock stars near the mid-century mark acting like
fourteen-year-olds?

We know that American men are in trouble down in
their bodies, down in the tissue. One source of help for
recovery from amnesia, for the awakening of the body, is the

re-discovery of the patriarch. Part of the alienation that men experience comes from being severed from their history, severed from their basic images or from the ground of their being.

This work attempts to connect men back to one aspect of this ground. The compass of this work is the archetypal figure or image of the patriarch. He is the guide, the direction giver and the subject of this undertaking, and to him it is dedicated.

An important discrimination can be made between types of patriarchy and "the patriarch." Traditional patriarchy is an attitude and an attempt to create an all-encompassing (economic, political, sexual, spiritual) system which aspires to domination by conscious control of all people, places and things both organic and inorganic. Patriarchy, from this point of view, can be adapted and practiced by men or women. Later I will define a kind of patriarchy ("homologous") which honors and respects other people and nature and seeks egalitarian relationships.

The patriarch, as I am using the term in this book, is an archetypal figure, one of the Eternal Ones who dwell in the psyche. An archetypal or essential image is a gift of human experience, a dowry of culture. Gifts expand our wealth, and they always carry a price both for giver and receiver. Part of the "givens" of culture—a gift received with contempt by many feminists and other writers by now—is the patriarch, his image and his influence.

Much of the way we have recognized ourselves has been influenced by this compass, the patriarch. How we have built our cities and houses and our body of knowledge, our forms of argumentation, our ways of thinking and behaving, what we often perceive as the bedrock of culture, and our understanding of Being itself have been affected strongly by the patriarch.

A compassionate and adequate apprehension of our history, both in terms of world events and of our inner, psychic heritage, will include an understanding of the patriarch. Seeing him as hostile, ruthless, dominating, many recent writers and thinkers have been sharply critical of his influence on the political, economic, interpersonal, sexual and familial spheres.

Jung writes:

> Just as all archetypes have a positive, favourable, bright side that points upwards, so also they have one that points downwards, partly negative and unfavourable, partly chthonic, but for the rest merely neutral (*CW* 9, i, ¶413).

If we are to see the richness of this figure, we must develop an empathy for the patriarch as a fundamental human experience, rather than as a rejected, worthless, no longer necessary part of our way of experiencing the world. What is rejected or scorned is often precisely that which is most important for psychological development. What is darkest, most hidden, most unacceptable to conscious awareness bears the seed of knowledge needed at that moment. A description of Christ in Matthew, a metaphor for Christ, is "the stone the builders rejected has become the cornerstone." Where we look inside ourselves and find shame, guilt, betrayal; where we find our desires to subordinate, control and exploit others—these are the areas where we can discover our full humanity. Merely to point at something, such as patriarchy, and say "I reject this" pushes it deeper into the unconscious, where it develops a more subtle and more intense power.

Modern men, like the legendary Odysseus, find themselves wandering lost in a world of monsters, wonders, impossibilities, treachery and threat, in their unconscious rather than in the mythic Mediterranean. They know, like Odysseus, that an important aspect of their being is their identity as father, as patriarch, as king. They long to return home. They are homeless, in distant seas.

2.

I suggest a model of two forms of patriarchy: "dualistic patriarchy" and "homologous patriarchy." The form that has received most condemnation from thinkers and writers of recent times is dualistic patriarchy.

Dualism sets one substance radically against another. In metaphysics, an example is the separation of mind and body in the work of Descartes, where mind is seen as one kind of substance or entity and body as a radically different kind. Dualism construes the opposites as polarized, not interchangeable, not to be confused with one another.

In dualistic patriarchy, there is always a need to find the opposite for the purpose of self-differentiation. Concepts therefore arise such as man *versus* woman, man *versus* the universe, time/eternity, animate/inanimate, superior/inferior, good/evil, left/right.

The ability to discriminate in opposites is essential for cognitive understanding, in the development of both intelligence and personal boundaries, and for the purpose of clarifying and solving certain types of problems. Even when we might know that the lines are not as clear as they seem, night and day, man and woman, mind and body all *are* opposites in some senses, and it is important for our social and intellectual acuity that we be able to distinguish such concepts, even if we understand that there is a lot of fuzzy area. Inside and outside of the body, for example, are extremely difficult to define at the orifices. If my mouth is open, my palate contacts the environment and may be defined as on the outside.

However, it is not dualisms themselves which cause a problem. In most cases it is not difficult to differentiate between, for example, a man and a woman. It *is* when various dualistic definitions get lined up together, such as man-good-right-superior-capable and woman-bad-inferior-left-incapable. This view ends in abuse and exploitation of those seen as "inferior" by those understood to be "superior."

"Homologous patriarchy" offers a different experience of the strength and wisdom of the father. A homologous view of the universe is one which does not set things apart and in conflict with one another, but sees reflection, similarity, parallel, echo, reverberation through all things. From this perspective, what is found in man will be found throughout the universe, and vice versa. Properties of mind are properties of body.

From a homologous point of view, what happens in the flesh happens on the earth. Links exist between human bone and stones, air and grass, blood and water, the eyes and the sun, mind and the moon, brain and clouds, skull and the rim of heaven.

A dualistic patriarchy is a pattern of prowess, competition and strength exercised for the exclusion of others for political, social and economic control. It is a format for gaining territory. It is highly charged, energetic, unafraid of violence. It is primarily a matter of offense and defense exercised out of a desire for controlling power. It is consumptive, directive, charging forward and causal. It has to do with rules, rightness, superiority, intransigence. It is penile in the sense that it focuses on the sexual organ as the center of control and power and literalizes that power as sexual.

Homologous patriarchy is a pattern of prowess, competition and strength exercised for the development of inner and outer man for the good of personal excellence, the health of the individual, of the family and of the community. Homologous patriarchy is not against the female but supports the value of the male body and the male self. It is self-reflective, open for comment. Homologous patriarchy is courageous and supports warrior values; the homologous patriarch values the collective and is conservationist in his view, since he sees the parallel between personal experience and that of others, and of the world and universe. Homologous patriarchy is acausal since it does not attempt to explain acts on the basis of a simple cause and effect relationship. It is phallic; it is erect for pleasure, production, creativity and relationships with others. The penis is seen more as a symbol for vigorous, charged, energy-seeking, creative joining and producing.

Homology is a model for men for the rediscovery of the patriarch. It must be noted, however, that an exploration of the world of archetypal imagery is full of traps for our thinking and awareness, for our imagination. All understanding drags ignorance in its wake as an essential seed. Distinctions such as the ones made here between dualistic and homologous patriarchy still pay homage—as all schisms, distinctions, clarifications do—to dualistic patriarchy. A placement of homologous patriarchy in a position of superiority over dualistic patriarchy is still dualistic. Any image is mixed and charged with possibilities and suggestions, some of which we may be privileged to see and "understand" but most of which we will not.

3.

We humans serve the archetype—or the Self, or God—not the other way around, and in this service we may discover our essential humanness, our history and our value beyond the personal limits of our own experience. One way to do this serving is through imagination, the primary modus operandi in this book.

"Patriarchal" ways of seeing and understanding the world arise from fundamental body experiences which are constant and immutable. Even an attempt to escape those constructs in human perception or thought will be strongly influenced by this background. Other images and structures, such as the Great Mother, the Goddesses, anima, the witch, will certainly have their effects upon the way we feel, think, imagine our lives and the world around us and, as "part of what we are given," comprise additional aspects of our essential humanness. The patriarch in both his negative and positive aspects continues to influence thought and perception even when there are self-conscious attempts to eliminate him.

The experience of compassion for what is essentially human in history and for "primitive material reverie, serene and lasting wisdom" (Bachelard) is best served through the nurturing of imagination itself, the direct expression of images that present themselves. The image does not submit to the logic of the ego; it cannot be grasped by simple and single-minded formulations, but suggests multiple and simultaneous meanings and values. A natural polytheism seems to apply in the psyche.

A mysterious and compelling ambiguity abides in the symbol. Jung defines symbol as "the best possible formulation of a relatively unknown thing." The poetic imagination invents and represents, and it indicates, by means of symbols, the texture and quality of experience, deepening our compassion and increasing our connection with what is fundamental in us, thus creating a psychology which serves the essential—archetypal psychology. A re-imagination of the patriarch is part of a re-imagination of the masculine; if it serves and attends to the symbolic and to the workings of the poetic imagination, it will reveal what is deeply masculine.

4.

A first association with the phrase "return to father" might be that of Jesus' parable of the prodigal son (Luke 15 : 11–24). The younger son of a rich father asks for his inheritance early. He squanders the money on harlots and revelry and is forced to return home broken and humiliated, ready to serve his father as hired help. The father instead receives him with deep love, gratitude and joy. But, steady and practical, the elder brother, who has stayed home and labored faithfully, is infuriated at the reception. The father remarks that his younger son "is as one returned from the dead" and thus deserves the best treatment and special attentions.

The two brothers incarnate on the one hand the desire to separate from father and on the other hand the desire to stay with father forever: these are contraries which cohabit in each man's being. Perhaps Jesus told the parable to allegorize God's unreasonable benevolence and forgiveness. Another element in the parable is to be found in the father's stinginess with the son who has stayed behind, the elder "good" son, who complains that, though the father has called for the fatted calf to be slaughtered for the younger brother, he didn't even give the elder son a goat to feast on with his friends.

A "return to father," learning again to embrace the best features of the patriarch, entails a turning back, seeking refuge and forgiveness. We may learn forgiveness from the patriarch and see ourselves in the desire to reunite which the prodigal himself feels. Men today seek a resolution and reconnection with the father, and stories of the uniting and forgiving between father and son can help show us how to accomplish this reunion.

At the same time, the elder brother aspect, that steady, practical quality in us, requires the stirring, driving anger that the return of the prodigal excites in him to provoke and maintain the separateness from father necessary to personal maturity. We must not be blind to the injustices of favoritism either, to the abuses which have been committed by the patriarchs.

The youngest son's connection with good fortune is a familiar theme in fairy tales, folktales, legends and everyday life. We often meet a youngest son who goes by such names as "Noodle," "Boots," "Jack." Often the youngest of three, he frequently has—despite a kind of goofiness, naivete and apparently all the wrong qualities for success—a basic kindness, personal warmth and integrity which find him fortune even in the face of his "shortcomings." He has a special relationship with the patriarchal father. He is able to triumph over trolls, to get the princess to laugh, to tame the untamable animals, to befriend the mute, the lame, the ridiculous; he can accomplish tasks which those with skill, knowledge and experience cannot.

In one story, "Boots and His Brothers," a man had three sons, Peter, Paul and John. John was "Boots," the youngest. They were extremely poor. The king's palace was nearby, and the king had two problems. An oak on the grounds was so big it took all the light from the palace. No one could chop it back: when one chip was chopped, two grew in its place. The king also had no well. He promised that whoever could cut the oak and dig a well would have the princess and half the kingdom.

Many tried and failed. The brothers walked to the palace to attempt the tasks. They heard chopping in the woods. "Boots" wondered aloud, "What is all that sound up yonder?" Having heard axmen working their entire lives, the brothers made fun of Boots: "You know very well what that is." "Just the same," said Boots, "I am going to look." He found an axe cutting by itself at the base of a tree. "Good day," he said. "Chopping here all by yourself, are you?"

"Yes, I have been chopping a long time waiting for you," said the axe. "Here I am," said Boots. He took the axe and put the head and handle in his pocket. His brothers teased him when he returned to them and asked what he had found of such great importance up in the woods. "Only an axe," answered Boots.

The brothers continued walking. They heard a digging, shoveling sound. "I wonder what that sound is," said Boots. "Oh, aren't you clever?" his brothers jeered at him. "As if you have never heard someone digging roots." Boots answered, "Anyway, I think it would be fun to see what it is."

So he set off again up the hillside, his brothers insulting him at his back.

When he got up the hillside a ways, he saw a spade digging and shoveling on its own. "Hello," said Boots cheerfully. "So you stand here digging and shoveling all day long?" "Yes," answered the spade. "Just digging and shoveling away, waiting for you to come along." "Well, here I am," answered Boots. He wrapped up the spade and brought it with him. Peter and Paul winked at each other and said, "Well, did you solve the great mystery? What did you find?" "Only a spade," answered Boots.

Walking further, they came to a brook. Thirsty, they stopped for a drink and a short rest. "I wonder where all this water comes from?" wondered Boots aloud. "I wonder if you are insane," said Peter. Paul laughed, "If you are not insane already, you will certainly be crazy soon. Where does a brook come from? My Lord, what a stupid question! Don't you understand how water comes from a spring?"

"Yes," said Boots. "But I would still like to see what it looks like." So, to the howlings of his brothers, he set off upstream. "What a numbskull!"

Soon Boots saw a great, large walnut with water trickling out of it. "Good day," he said. "So you lie here trickling, running water all alone all day?" "Yes I do, yes sir. I have been lying here trickling for a long time waiting for you to come along." "Here you have me," said Boots. He took a clump of moss to plug the hole so the water would not run out and ran down to join his brothers.

"Well, what rare, wondrous thing have you discovered now?" Peter and Paul jeered. "Oh, only a hole with water running out of it." Shaking their heads, the older brothers picked themselves up and said, "Let's be off. Enough nonsense." "After all, I had the fun of seeing where the water comes from," offered Boots.

Arriving finally at the king's palace, they found that the oak had grown to twice its original size, two chips growing for every one chopped away. Peter and Paul were not dismayed or surprised, but, certain of their abilities, each in turn started hacking away at the oak. But they suffered the same fate as the others, and the oak did nothing but grow and shade the palace more. The king's guard stopped them as soon as possible. Then Boots asked for his turn. "Save yourself the bother," said the king, angry at Peter and Paul. "Well, I would just like to try anyway, please." The king conceded, "Well, you can't do any worse than your brothers."

Boots took the axe head out of his pocket and put it on the handle. "Hack away," he told the axe, which began chopping in a wild fury, the chips flying everywhere. The oak quickly groaned, tottered and fell. That being done, Boots unwrapped the spade and said, "Dig in." The spade dug up a storm until the earth and rock flew out of a grand hole; soon the well was dug. The well being as big and deep as he wished, he took out the walnut, laying it in the corner of the well, pulling loose the plug. "Trickle and run," he said. The water fairly gushed out, till a fine big stand of water stood by the castle.

Boots had felled the oak shading the king's palace and had provided a well, so he got the princess and half the kingdom, as the king had promised. Peter and Paul stood scratching their heads in utter amazement. They turned to each other and decided between themselves that perhaps Boots had not been insane after all when he took to wondering.

This story, like many "youngest brother" stories, shows the special relationship between the patriarchal father—

here the king—and the youngest and most naive son. It is the wonderment, the reverie, the curiosity which lead Boots to discovery, not the logic of the older brothers, Peter and Paul. Wonderment opens possibilities of discovery and the possibilities of a relationship with the patriarchal king, who offers half of his kingdom, his territory, and his daughter, his young femininity, to Boots.

A connection of this kind is frequently found in folktales. The patriarch maintains the kingdom but needs help, which can only come from the youngest and least likely source. His well has dried up. Vice versa, the youngest son needs the patriarch, the king, in order to have his share of the kingdom, to have territory and a marriage. The two are joined and related to each other. They require each other.

Wondering by itself, without a goal or purpose, has no ground, no place. We can see this, because up to the time of the beginning of the tale, Boots's inquisitiveness had not resulted in a richness. Father and sons were poor. On the other hand, the king is sequestered in his palace without light and without water. His source has dried up.

The patriarch is both warm and cold (a theme to be discussed in detail in chapter two). In this story he appears to have dried up and to be in the dark. He is seeking an answer through rather rigidly prescribed tasks. Someone else is to come cut the tree and make the well and fill it. Yet he is willing to be generous—to share his kingdom and his daughter, to offer of what he has.

5.

An even more striking example of the combination of coldness and warmth joined together in the patriarch is found in the story of Abraham and Isaac. When the ancient Abraham was one hundred years old and his wife Sara was ninety-one, she gave birth to a son, Isaac. To test Abraham's faith, God ordered him to sacrifice the boy. When he was clearly ready to do so, with the knife at the ready, God substituted a ram, the traditional sacrifice, for the boy.

We would say that Abraham's faith in God was absurd, insane. That he would trust God in this way is crazy, impossible. The ancient patriarch Abraham, old and brittle, becomes father to new life and to something absurd, irrational and impossible. God's request—that he commit, or be ready to commit, the unthinkable—is the very source of a new integration.

6.

There is also a time to "turn one's back on the father," on the personal father, and to seek the mentor, the teacher, the master. The great fifteenth-century Italian humanist Marsilio Ficino writes that, of the 'nine guides' of the young student of life, the three earthly ones are ". . . a father who is prudent, a teacher who is excellent, and a doctor who is brilliant" (p. 3). Such qualities, first experienced in another, older man, allow the young person to model and discover values and meaning. Such tutelary qualities of the *patris*— the father, whether he wears the hat of the teacher, doctor or man of commerce—are those which in traditional societies helped the young encounter what is primal and valuable, as we will see in the next chapter.

Men's House

In many of the ancient societies we know about, our fore-fathers constructed a house for men apart from women. The young man fathomed there what it meant to belong to the group "men" and unraveled the puzzle of women and their ways from the elders' teachings. The older man found therein companionship; a barrack filled with stories of hunting, commerce and war; a retreat for a man among other men; and the opportunity for the pride of giving the teachings to younger men and boys.

The kiva, constructed by the Pueblo Indians, the sweat lodge used throughout Europe as well as by the American Indians, and the initiation hut made by the Australian and other 'aborigines' are sacred spaces dedicated to men. These are the places where boys became men, where they separated from the women and children into a 'place apart.' Time spent in the initiation hut or the men's house held a particular meaning—the meaning of a fellowship among males that could be gotten only in these places set apart from the other buildings in the village.

The kivas are circular or rectangular, with timbered roofs. One enters the kiva from the hatchway by descending a ladder. The floor is well-chosen sandstone slabs, and the walls are set with carefully finished fine masonry. A dais adorns one end of the room, a fire pit is placed in the middle, and the *shipapu* at the other end. The latter is the place of emergence of men and animals into our world. The walls are painted and designed with sacred images telling stories. Women are not allowed to enter the kiva except to bring food. The men's house is for their special ceremonies, for lounging among men and for weaving or painting the Gods and events of the world.

Other "initiation huts," whether made of long timbers such as those of the American Northwest Indians, from sticks, leaves and mud such as those of the Bornean aborigines, or bricks and mortar as in the twelfth-century bridge-building guilds of Europe, represent a "place made sacred" for men. Whatever the form or material, these places were designed, built and decorated by men on the instructions of their grandfathers, instructions passed through the stories told through the generations.

Initiation into the world of men in traditional cultures was an event of primary importance, not only in the life of the individual boy, but also of the family and of the tribe. In many cultures we know of, elaborate and often gory celebrations of coming into manhood took place. Through often painful rituals full of physical torture—including circumcision, subincision of the penis or other parts of the body, even knocking a tooth out—the death of the boy was made vivid. His mother and the other women of the tribe threatened at a distance to engulf him again into their world; with wild shouts, groans, laments and grieving they tried to call him back into their nest. But the men protected and pulled the boy to them, claiming him as one of them, one of the men of the tribe.

The voices, words, stories and images of men and the masculine in this house are our subject. We also speak of women and the feminine, because in the men's house both are important, although clear distinctions are made between the genders.

It is a source of pride to be a man in the men's house, to enjoy masculine qualities and not shrivel from nature. Joking and roughhousing enliven the men's house, arguments break out sometimes, and not infrequently moments of silence, suffering and weeping settle on the men, possibly followed soon by a new outbreak of joking, probably sexual in reference. Though somehow the perfidious story spread that men don't cry or are against it, it is not true. Men may not cry in the office or on the flight line, but they do in the men's house when they experience sorrow, sadness and grief for the failures and wounds of the tribe.

In fact, the glue that binds men together, that brings them together is often loss, the memory of what once was. Men gather when they have lost a wife, divorced a wife, lost a job, lost custody of the children. But more frequently they congregate to lament the loss of youth. Veterans of war come together. The old team reassembles. Buddies from school gather.

On these occasions they tell the stories; they live again "the times." Telling these stories itself is an invitation to the God Eros, the male God of relationships, to attend the mystery of the telling.

One version of the birth of Eros is that he is born of his mother Chaos. Russell Lockhart writes,

> The birth of Eros from Chaos is an important image. Frequently our lives become chaos, a relationship

enters or re-enters the chaos stage. Our experience descends into darkness with nothing to hang onto, all things become black and disconnected. Relationship frequently brings chaos or pulls us into the gaping chasm of chaos. . . . We can get lost and devastated in the chaos of relationship. Yet if myth be right, if myth carries an archetypal truth, then chaos carries a seed which, if nurtured and allowed time to come to birth, becomes Eros in us. Chaos is for the purpose of bringing in, giving birth to a new connection to life, giving birth to the very principle of creative connection, giving birth to Eros. . . . Chaos must be borne, it is the burden, the unwanted thing. Chaos must be borne to give Eros birth. The mythology of Eros tells us that this god embodies the spirit of relatedness. (P. 125)

Lockhart continues, "Eros, then, is the god of relationship. To relate means to bring elements, particularly humans, into some form of connection. . . . Eros means telling."

One male mystery is the simple fact of telling stories, telling one's life in images and events in the presence of others. Fishing stories, hunting stories, stories of conquest, stories of sports events, stories of relationships, of old friends, of schooltimes, of adventures, of car accidents, of drunken nights, the stories of lives and times gone by. The "old boy system" is a network of stories among men. The stories of kids once playing in the streets together now become the stories of old men owning those streets.

So many stories! "I lost my job," "I had to cross the picket lines," "my wife left me," "my kid won't go to school," "another guy got the promotion," "I had a windfall on the market,"

"Marie is pregnant," "We lost the playoffs," "I had a huge bass on the line and lost him."

Women have at times accused men of "not being open with their feelings"; they say that men only "tell the story." Although the expression of emotion, of "inner feelings," can heighten or clarify relatedness between people, it is the telling of the stories—the chaos of life formed and told—that gives birth to Eros.

One epithet of Eros is "limb relaxer." Telling stories, telling one's life, relaxes the limbs. Sorrow and grief shared no longer have to be carried in tension in the limbs, tension in the muscles. The 'rigid patriarch' is loosened in the telling and with the moistness of tears is even further softened and relaxed. His well, dried up, is filled by young Boots with his walnut-spring. Talking of losses of youth and asking for help, as the king did in the story "Boots," is a way of drawing new sources, a way of moistening and filling up the dryness.

A Men's House is a sacred container, a mysterious vessel. Among women, the expression of feeling is more "normal," ordinary; not less valuable, but part of our customary experience, part of "what we expect." When Mary, mother of Jesus, weeps, we are not surprised. We read with astonishment that Jesus weeps.

The connection between women, the unconscious and mystery has often been made. Men and the masculine have been associated with consciousness, clarity, logic and directness and therefore have been believed to be knowable. This is not what we discover in the men's house, for even if the connection between men and these qualities were shown to be incontestable, is consciousness not itself a great and unplumbed mystery? William James has uttered the bafflingly self-negating statement "I believe that 'consciousness' . . . is the name of a nonentity, and has no right among first principles." This appears in his essay "Does 'Consciousness' Exist?"

There *is* a realm of predictable and stereotyped masculine behavior typified by a cold and unfeeling violence toward nature, woman and man. And there is a warm and fervent, philanthropic and bighearted *paterfamilias* which cohabits in each man's being with the glacial, impartial killer. There is mystery here and much unexplored terrain. When we use a word like "macho" to describe a man, a phrase like "masculine power structure" or "patriarchal" to describe a system of thought or political stance, "male-dominated" to describe a profession, or "sexist" to describe an attitude, such expressions are, thanks to the bold denunciations of the women's movement, woven into our current vocabulary in a way that may lead us to believe we understand what we are saying.

A historical interpretation of a fact—such as that few women appear in history books credited with major political influence during war times—seems to enforce and demonstrate a point of view, e.g., that men have kept women from taking their rightful place in creating political influence. An interpretation may lead us to believe that we understand a fact and what it means. We might conclude, for example, that men don't like, respect or trust women and thus have kept them from exercising their proper political role. Such a perspective only allows a narrow understanding of what the meaning of the facts is and may be more deluding than informative about men and their beliefs and feelings or about women and their beliefs and feelings. We simply don't know the range of meaning; we cannot conclude that we divine the sum and substance of a historical "fact." A perspective which allows us the greatest access to the center or foundation and also to the periphery of what men and the masculine are will remain an open container, a semi-porous vessel with membranes through which may pass not only a current and seemingly sage interpretation of men and the masculine, but also images and wisdom which have come from our own old blood, the guts of human experience, images which might jolt and shake us, might seem insensitive or ugly (according to current taste), or beautiful but strange and not appropriate.

One feminist writer describes the "demonic influence of patriarchy" (Schneiders, p. 52). The presence of evil in all affairs and an acceptance of such evil are a prerequisite to a full human experience. Yes, there may be a demonic influence of patriarchy, but is a bull only his horns? A denial of violence, malice and evil is a rejection of our tissue. Cain pulsates as strongly as Abel in all of us, as do Judas Iscariot, Genghis Khan, and Saul, Son of Kish, David, Solomon and Nitar. Piety does little but inflame the prostate, infect the bladder, shallow the breath, beleaguer digestion.

Regardless of whatever desire we may have to banish him, the patriarch flows in our visceral and psychic history blended of goodwill, malice, and neutrality and shades of these. As with any archetypal image, an 'anatomy' of the patriarch may be sketched, yet such an operation is best done as an exercise in reverie and suggestion of essences, since our vision is but dim. Whatever argument made for or against our love of the patriarch is perhaps best entered in a state of self-mordancy, self-satire, irony. As the patriarch wears a many-colored "Joseph's coat" and speaks with many tones, so a reverie about him will have many voices and languages to emblematize him with words.

Dreamer, dream interpreter, braggart, foreteller of his own great fortune, his father's favorite son, the biblical Joseph lorded it over his brothers. When his father Jacob gave him a many-colored coat, the brothers were fed up. They cast Joseph into a pit, sold him into slavery and returned a bloodied coat to Jacob, suggesting Joseph was killed and eaten by animals.

Slave Joseph was sold to Potiphor, high official of Pharaoh. Potiphor's wife brewed a lust for the handsome slave, who had leveraged his way into overseeing the house; he refused his master's wife and, framed, wound up in jail. There he garnered fame interpreting dreams, including two important ones involving Pharaoh. The impressed Pharaoh granted Joseph a lordly position in the realm.

Again interpreting important dreams and signs, Joseph saved grain against drought and famine, selling it at good profits in a very bad year. His vengeful brothers had to come into Egypt to buy food. Joseph recognized them and set a trap to get his father to come to him. He demanded that they return and bring back the youngest brother, Benjamin, who had been left behind with father Jacob. The brothers returned with Benjamin; Joseph planted his own silver drinking and divining cup in Benjamin's luggage, thinking he could arrest Benjamin and get his father to come beg for the boy's release. The oldest brother, Judah, pleaded with Joseph, saying that if they returned to the father without Benjamin—Jacob's favorite son since the loss of his dear Joseph—the father would surely die of grief.

In the end, Joseph broke down and revealed his identity out of sympathy for the father. Jacob was sent for, and the tribe came to Egypt and settled in Gosham.

The brothers, out of their envy, had betrayed the father and taken from him the son whom he most cherished. Again we see the connection between the favored son, that son most loved by the father, and the patriarch. Brash and naive, Joseph was a dreamer, an interpreter of dreams. Certainly, his self-absorption, self-confidence and lording it over his siblings to the delight of the father did not hold him in good stead with them. He is rejected, sold and gotten rid of.

The youngest son aspect of the patriarch—youthful exuberance and power—has been stripped away from him. The many-colored coat, which we think of when we talk of Joseph, represents a vibrancy, multiplicity, what we might call his "homologous nature." It is a symbol of masculine creativity. Joseph seems to have that fine balance, as we see throughout his life, between the things of the inner world—interpretation of dreams, understanding of symbols and images, intuition—and the ability to manage the affairs of the outer world: business and commerce. He effectively predicts the drought and famine: he is in touch with the natural world. And he efficiently plans how to supply the resources he and his tribe will need during the famine.

We see that, in the time of great famine, father Jacob and the other sons are without supplies. This is reminiscent of the king in the "Boots" story. In that tale, we remember, the well had dried up. In this case, the grain is no longer available—without the son who is the dreamer, the intuitive, the one in touch with the things of the inner and outer worlds; without that bragging son, who is impetuous, full of himself and his prowess.

Pharaoh recognizes this connection—between the world psyche and individual psyche—in promoting Joseph out of slavery into a high official place in the kingdom. It is Joseph who, like Boots, adds the element of illogic, the world of wonder and dreams, to the well-being of the community.

The need of a father for a favorite is demonstrated in the fact that Jacob kept Benjamin, the youngest son, home with him. He had a particularly protective attitude toward Benjamin. The reunion of Joseph, his brothers and the father Jacob and their establishment of a settlement in Egypt define a new era of patriarchy. Now Joseph combines in himself the qualities of his own personal father, who represents a nurturing and good-willed gullibility; of the kingly father or true patriarch, Pharaoh, who represents the highest powers, the apogee of hierarchy and subordination of others; of his brothers, who represent greed, labor, envy, ordinary vision; and of his own person, representing primarily vigor, endurance, a combining of the inner and outer worlds, and the ability to unite and hold the family in times of duress and difficulty.

The Patriarch
Images from Various Writers

A classical image of the patriarch that comes from Greco-Roman sources is that of Kronos or Saturn. James Hillman treats this figure at some length in his essay on "Senex and Puer." He writes,

> Let us begin with a prayer to Saturn, an Arabic one from the *Picatrix* of the tenth century, which circulated widely in the late Middle Ages of Western Europe:

>> O Master of sublime name and great power, supreme Master; O Master Saturn: Thou, the Cold, the Sterile, the Mournful, the Pernicious; Thou, whose life is sincere and whose word sure; Thou, the Sage and Solitary, the Impenetrable; Thou, whose promises are kept; Thou who art weak and weary; Thou who hast cares greater than any other, who knowest neither pleasure nor joy; Thou, the old and cunning, master of all artifice, deceitful, wise, and judicious; Thou who bringest prosperity or ruin and makest men to be happy or unhappy! I conjure Thee, O Supreme Father, by Thy great benevolence and Thy generous bounty, to do for me what I ask. . . .

Appropriately, our starting point is duplex. Saturn-Kronos is on one hand

> . . . a benevolent God of agriculture, . . . the ruler of the Golden Age when men had abundance of all things, . . . the lord of the Islands of the Blessed, . . . and the building of cities. . . . On the other hand he was the gloomy, dethroned, and solitary god conceived as "dwelling at the uttermost end of land and sea," "exiled . . .," "ruler of the nether gods" . . . prisoner or bondsman in . . . Tartarus, . . . the god of death and the dead. On the one hand he was the father of gods and men, on the other hand the devourer of children, eater of raw flesh, the consumer of all, who "swallowed up all the gods". . . .

According to the Warburg Institute's authoritative study of Saturn, in no Greek god-figure is the dual aspect so real, so fundamental, as in the figure of Kronos, so that even with the later additions of the Roman Saturn who "was originally not ambivalent but definitely good," the compounded image remains at core bi-polar. Saturn is at once archetypal image for wise old man, solitary sage, the *lapis* as rock of ages with all its positive moral and intellectual virtues, *and* for the Old King, that castrating castrated ogre. He is the world as building of cities *and* the not-world of exile. At the same time that he is father of all he consumes all; by living on and from his fatherhood he feeds himself insatiably from the bounty of his own paternalism. *Saturn is image for both positive and negative senex.* (1979, pp. 15–16)

Once we move away from a view of the patriarch which would reduce him to a single interpretation, we can begin to see the richness possible in what was formerly seen as an "evil" to be eradicated. We need the experience of Kronos or Saturn; our psyche needs and hungers for the experience represented by such a figure as an essential aspect of the fullness of human being.

The word "patriarch" means "a father who rules his family or tribe" and comes from the Greek *patriarchos*, "father of a race," *patros*, "father, lineage," and *archos*, "leader." It is interesting to note that the "patri" part of the word "patriarch" can be related either to *patros*, father, or to *patria*, family. Thus, it can be read that the "father is the family" or "the family is the father," if we see the terms as both having a place in the prefix.

Another way to see this image is that family = father, so that whatever associations one has to father—say, authority, organizing, power as a kind of father principle—are indeed what the father is. The fathering, organizing principle in the family is intimately connected to and responsible for the structuring and organizing that all cultures have expressed forever, namely, kinship, and the structuring of human relationship on the basis of certain "rules." Thus, the patriarch is, quoting the definition above, "a father who rules a family" but, restated in these terms, is also a "family (*patria*) which rules a family" or "the inherent principle of a family which rules a family."

The word "rules" is important to look at in this regard. Though we often associate a certain negativity to the verb "rule," such as in the idiom "he rules it over her," the word itself does not require such connotations. "Rule" comes from the Latin *regulare*, "to direct, regulate," from Latin *regula*, which is "a straight piece of wood." The Latin verb form *regere* means "to keep straight, lead, or direct." When we say that a father "rules a family" or "family principle rules a family," we are saying that there is direction, leading and a straightening which are measured against a straight piece of wood, an image with strong reference to carpentry and building.

The word "family" derives originally from an Indo-European base *dh-mo,* which means "house," and this base *dh-mo* is an enlargement from a further base *dhe* which means "to put, place; to do, make." There is in the word "family," then, an organic reference to a structure, a house, and to the making or placing of that house. Such activities involve carpentry (or masonry, etc.; an activity related to carpentry in that it is a making of a structure, whose material is less important than the activity) and a measuring and creating on the basis of certain general principles which may be applied in quite varied ways. Witness the incredible variations in human dwelling which are all related in principle to very basic designs—actually to the square, the circle and the triangle at root.

In one account of the origins of Eros, referred to above, he is the son of Chaos. He is the binding God, the God of connectedness. From the unformed, Chaos, comes the former, Eros. Eros is generally known in Greek stories as a God who does not come in the form of a particular personality but creates a certain "feel" or "quality." One knows when Eros has been present. We see the effects rather than the actual presence of the God. He creates an energy, a vibrant, excitatory phenomenon between people.

What binds men to each other often has to do with what Aristotle termed "Virtue"—*arete,* which involves acting, creating, doing good. Friends, according to Aristotle, spend time together doing things for the good of the other as well as for one's own good. Fellowship is the joining together for the good of others as well as for oneself.

Experience together makes a place where this connection, this binding, can take place: we invite Eros. Friendship between men frequently comes about through shared activities: sailing, commerce, designing, mountain climbing, performing, athletics, drinking, traveling. Our expression of masculinity, as well as a sense of shared values, arises from these activities. The Eros quality comes into relationships often not in quiet friendships of peaceful moments shared in the lull of the evening but in energetic action creating, producing within the realm of *homo faber:* man the maker.

Eros, separated from his quality of binding people together sexually, carries a certain dynamism of his own, which can feel sexual. Dan Ackroyd spoke of this quality in John Belushi:

> I am not a homo and neither was John. But when I saw him come into a room, I got the jump you get when you see a beautiful girl. It was that kind of feeling. It was that adrenaline, that pit of the stomach rush. He was always exciting to be around. One knew that something was going to happen, even if it was just a matter of taking a walk. Being with him was electric, really electric. (Michaelis, p. 276)

In male relationships, one may see the masculine face of Eros bringing his fire. Inspired by his audacity to confront social definitions, men are bound by Eros to their strength and power. There is even a certain fatality or destructiveness which must be recognized in the dynamism inspired by Eros; men sometimes do crazy things together, dangerous and even with a sense of "self-destructiveness." There is a danger in the "dare" and also a form of love.

The arrows of Eros are strong and accurate, penetrating the lives of men with a sense of divinity. Eros among men inspires a warrior quality, a quality of joining together for action, commitment, to make an impact on themselves and on others.

What of those who are broken, wounded, undermined, betrayed, fallen men—as we all are in some way? Another God, Hephaistos, may be called for us in these circumstances. Son of noble parents, Hephaistos was ignoble, a cuckold, a limping cripple. Thrown off Mount Olympus because his mother thought him ugly, he fell and became lame. His malformed legs caused him to walk awkwardly. The other Gods howled with laughter at him. Hera, his mother, kept him out of sight because of his deformation. Later he was cuckolded by Aphrodite, his wife, and her lover Ares. Still, as a God, he remained bound to the house of the Gods. He was patron of artists, craftsmen and mechanics. Strong, bearded, a great hulking blacksmith, he worked at joining, at artistry, at craftsmanship. He created beauty out of the ugliness of his own body, parallel to the forming of Eros out of Chaos.

From the woundedness of humiliation, Hephaistos formed objects of great beauty. He created golden palaces for the Gods. Striking his father Zeus on the head with his hammer to alleviate a headache, he served as midwife to Athene, who sprang out of that august head. Though he stood under other Gods, he forged a place in their community. Thus he is our patron in our woundedness and crippledness.

He inspires and challenges us, as a good father might, to over-come our self-pity, rage and blaming—to "make something of ourselves."

"Power" means etymologically "ability" and "structure," "a doing or making or creating." Therefore, a masculine power structure is an ability for making or constructing or, alternatively, a created or creative ability. A masculine power structure may in these terms be said to be the father who builds the structure, a principle of organizing and measuring and making of the family, the house. These are the qualities mentioned by Hillman in speaking of Saturn as " 'the ruler of the Golden Age when men had abundance of all things . . . the lord of the Islands of the Blessed . . . and the building of cities.' "

As Hillman indicates, however, Saturn-Kronos is not only "the world as builder of cities" but also the "not-world of exile." And certainly, as Hillman writes, a system built with too rigid a structure may participate in this aspect of dead-liness carried by the Kronos image: "At the same time that he is father of all he consumes all; by living on and from his fatherhood he feeds himself insatiably from the bounty of his own paternalism." The crux of the matter is that the two aspects go together and require each other. Without the deadliness and the consumption, there is no building; with-out the power, there is no structure; no ruin, no prosperity. The paterfamilias carries the specific image of the patriarch in the family, and, as anyone knows from personal experi-ence, the personal father often well demonstrates the Satur-nian "image of both positive and negative senex."

Sherwood Anderson, in his autobiography (in Firestone, pp. 30–39), eloquently expresses the ambivalence of love and fear that the child feels in the presence of a powerful and mysterious father. He describes his father as a storyteller, a liar who would pretend to be anything he wanted to be to get his way (like Saturn, " 'master of all artifice, deceitful, wise, and judicious' "), but who had the respect of even the most dignified members of the community and frequently met with a group late at night on the porch, entertaining them and speaking with them of all things (" 'the ruler of the Golden Age when men had abundance of all things' "). Sherwood himself as a boy felt utterly subjected to his father's powerful presence (as Saturn-Kronos, " 'on the one hand he was the father of gods and men, on the other hand the devourer of children, eater of raw flesh, the consumer of all, who swallowed up all the gods' "). Anderson writes:

> A boy wants something very special from his father. You are always hearing it said that fathers want their sons to be what they feel they cannot themselves be, but I tell you it also works the other way. I know that, as a small boy, I wanted my father to be a proud silent dignified one. When I was with other small boys and he passed along the street, I wanted to feel in my breast the flow of pride. (Firestone, pp. 30–31)

His father does not comply, of course, with the hidden wishes of the boy; he does not know them and would not conform to them in any case, since he is very fully his own man.

The secret which is revealed a few pages later in the autobiography is that Sherwood deeply desires to enter somehow in that realm of his father of which he is king, the men's house. Then one night, his father very uncharacteristically enters the house in silence, with a strange, purposeful look on his face, very frightening to Sherwood, who lies falling asleep but suddenly very awake in his bed.

His father takes him out into the night, away from the mother. In a ritualistic scene reminiscent in its symbolism of traditional initiation rites, he takes Sherwood to a pond; the two of them strip down and swim together in silence, fulfilling a strangely ceremonial necessity. Anderson describes his ambivalent feelings as his father comes to get him, "I was afraid and then, right away, I wasn't afraid" (ibid., p. 37). The two returned to the house in silence, and a bond was formed between them. Anderson became, as we know, a famous storyteller and liar of sorts, winning fame for his inventiveness and ability to evoke the story suited well to the porch and to the men's house. The identification with the building, creating dominance of father and the gifts of his arrogance, his power, sagacity and solitariness (Saturnian qualities) show him to be a stand-in for Kronos. He is a teller of timeless tales set clearly in time and place, in a specific house and town.

The qualities of direction, leading, ruling in the sense of the building of structure are perhaps nowhere more clearly and succinctly expressed than in a passage from Gurdjieff's *Meetings with Remarkable Men* in which he speaks of his father's influence on him:

> My father had a very simple, clear, and quite definite view on the aim of human life. He told me many times in my youth that the fundamental striving of every man should be to create for himself an inner freedom toward life and to prepare for himself a happy old age. He considered that the indispensability and imperative necessity of this in life was so obvious that it ought to be

understandable to everyone without any wiseacring. But a man could attain this aim only if, from childhood up to the age of eighteen, he had acquired data for the unwavering fulfillment of the following four commandments:

First—To love one's parents.

Second—To remain chaste.

Third—To be outwardly courteous to all without distinction whether they be rich or poor, friends or enemies, power-possessors or slaves, and to whatever religion they may belong, but inwardly to remain free and never to put much trust in anyone or anything.

Fourth—To love work for work's sake and not for its gain. (Gurdjieff, p. 39)

An emphasis is placed on autonomy, self-directedness and fulfillment for the individual, the child and the family. The relationship perceived by Gurdjieff is not one of his own inferiority, subordination or loss as a result of the vehemence of his father's insistence on a particular code or structure of patriarchal values. He writes, "My personal relationship to him was not as toward a father, but as toward an elder brother; and he, by his constant conversation with me and his extraordinary stories, greatly assisted the arising in me of poetic images and high ideals" (Gurdjieff, p. 40).

Again images of Saturn-Kronos arise: "the old and cunning master of all artifice, deceitful, wise, and judicious." The poetic images that Gurdjieff speaks of—artifice and deceit—arise within and, one may say, in conjunction with the "anchoring" of his "high ideals," the father direction which he so eloquently describes. Though poetic imagery and art have often been associated with the feminine, the unconscious and "lunar" effects, we see that a masculine, patriarchal father structure can just as easily be a source of creativity, intuition and invention.

The poet Robert Bly has turned back to ancient sources for a rediscovery of what he calls the "deep masculine" (Thompson, 1982, p. 34). The presence of the father and his influence on a child—especially a male—is powerfully expressed in his book of poems *The Man in the Black Coat Turns* (1981). A few lines from the poem "My Father's Wedding 1924" may give a sense of the power of the father's influence; the poem develops male images of wood, the body and familial relations.

> Today, lonely for my father, I saw
> a log, or branch,
> long, bent, ragged, bark gone.
> I felt lonely for my father when I saw it.
> It was the log
> that lay near my uncle's old milk wagon.
>
> Some men live with an invisible limp,
> stagger, or drag
> a leg. Their sons are often angry.
> Only recently I thought:
> Doing what you want . . .
> Is that like limping? Tracks of it show in sand.
>
> (P. 48)

Though this son experiences a number of emotions often called "negative"—anger, sadness, grief, frustration—and

Gurdjieff's relationship was expressed in terms of gratitude, great love and joy, the effect of the father's presence and influence on "poetic images" is similar in the two.

Whether the relationship with the father is sought literally or metaphorically, though, the job of the child is to find his autonomy, his own patriarchy—that is, his own family, his own house to rule and be ruled by. William Carlos Williams speaks of the difficulty of this breaking apart that must be sudden and powerful:

> That relationship between father and son is one of the toughest things in the world to break down. It seems so natural and it is natural—in fact, it's inevitable— but it separates as much as it joins. A man wants to protect his son, wants to teach him the things he, the father, has learned or thinks he has learned. But it's exactly that which a child resents. He wants to know but he wants to know on his own—and the longer the paternal influence lasts the harder it is to break down and the more two individuals who should have much in common are pushed apart. Only a sudden enforced break can get through that one. (In Firestone, p. 364)

In my reading and reverie on the words of Williams and other authors presented in these chapters, many words and images arise to describe fundamental experiences common to them. Two suggest themselves to me here as very important, which I call upon with the words "pattern" and "repair." The first tells us how to understand and know experience. The other tells us how we can respond when there is a rupture, a breakdown, a failure.

These two words arise, as we shall see, from the two roots of "patriarch"—one meaning "father" and the other meaning "country" or "family." Both are helpful in our full understanding of patriarch and add richness to our sense of the meaning of the father/family structure which rules or guides us.

Part II: dh-mo

The Father Is the House
Excursions on Language, on the Images of Pattern and Repair, and on the Archetypal Father Warrior

Human life is language or at the very least is unfathomable without words. Even Abbott Anthony, who wandered in Judea for thirty years never speaking to another person, carried on endless conversations with God in nine idioms. Whether in the *very* beginning was the word—Logos—who can know? Yet in the beginning of everything *we* can know was the word.

What brought us into material being was the mother, her body. What brought us to know that body was logos—the father. What fathers human *experience*, then, is the word, joining with matter. Mother's body, personal and archetypal—and her own knowledge and wisdom—communicates sensate being, breath, pulsation, our first experience of boundary. Mother's wisdom and teaching continue through life in the bond which resonates with her son. Father—and here we speak of both the patriarch and the personal father—ignites knowing, awareness, consciousness: the word as tool, weapon, forge, foundation.

A God of "making" and the Word is Wodin, the divine Nordic patriarch. He carries on his shoulders the two ravens Hugin ("Thought") and Munin ("Memory"), who fly to the end of creation daily to bring back knowledge. Heroic, stern, Wodin is mainly concerned with battle. Yet he is responsible for poetry, inspiration and the runes. He hangs on the World Tree, Yggdrassil, for nine days, gazing into the depths of hell to learn to write the runes. He nearly loses his life securing the poetic elixir and makes a trip to hell to find the answer to one question. He sits under the gallows to absorb knowledge. He is known as wily, untrustworthy and deceitful. Consciousness is dangerous.

Consciousness is the sin of Adam, who blames Eve. But Eve rightly blames the serpent, who himself is only an agent of Logos—the word—speaking into her ear. Once created, the word cannot resist being spoken. Thus God, the father, offers the hapless choice of life without consciousness, the womb where all is darkness, unseparated and undiscriminated, or life with awareness, sin, suffering and doubt, joy, pleasure and transcendence. No culture has ever chosen the void, though it cannot be denied that some individuals attempt to return there as a response to the extreme rawness of knowledge.

Perhaps we shall never know whether thought fathers language or language fathers thought, but we do know that sons become fathers, so language and thought may be known as lineal progenitors of what we know and say. And what we think and speak is loaded always with the inscrutably rich layers of experience of Adam's innumerable brood.

To understand the patriarchal father requires that we understand language. This is perhaps tantamount to stating that we can never understand him, for who can fathom language? More suited to our raw brutality may be the goal of proximate appreciation of language, the application of rough rules and gazing with wonder on the richly layered depth of words. A father builds a house for his family as his best, meager attempt to mimic the image of heaven, a place of safety, warmth, protection and love. Thus we attempt to understand language, a universal and divine phenomenon, by building a temple to invite the word; we appreciate and stand under the awning of language.

Our textbook is the word, and our dictionary is speech of all possible types. Words carry their own meaning, carry their own history; words father themselves and father thought. A dictionary is a "book of sayings" (Latin *diction-arius*) and therefore a quarry of human speech. The roots of the word "dictionary" have to do with digits, fingers, which point out what we say; words point us out to ourselves and show us what we think of ourselves. Words grant consciousness and therefore father us.

The word "pattern" is defined as "(1) a person or thing so ideal as to be worthy of imitation or copying, (2) a model, guide, plan, etc., used in making things, (3) the full-scale model used in making a sand mold for casting metal, (4) something representing a type; example; sample, (5) an arrangement of form; disposition of parts or elements; design or decoration: as wallpaper patterns, the pattern of a novel, (6) definite direction, tendency or characteristics; as, behavior patterns" (*Webster's New World Dictionary*). The word arises from Middle English *patron,* which comes from *patronus,* "protector," and before that from Latin *patris,* "of the father." Thus, it may be said that the father is the pattern but also that "the pattern is the father"; by this I mean once again that the organizing, building—the carpentry—of human experience may be called "fathering" or that "patterning is fathering."

This patterning I call "fathering" is not necessarily something to be practiced only by men; yet to the man, whose archetypal sexual pattern is modeled long before he ever enters the men's house (and some men do not enter there), such a pattern is, and always was, factored and fathered in him innately, biographically, biologically (what has testicles and penis tends to father) and culturally through the metaphor and image structures of our civilizations. For the female, such a pattern is always culturally learned if learned at all. This is not a comment on the value or genuine ability of either sex in its individuals to exercise the patriarchal qualities.

A central thread running through this book is the tension between ancient—and sometimes rigidified—forms of language, thinking, creation, building and the idiosyncrasy of individual proclivity. There are forms which are immutably connected to enhancing and mirroring the fullness or richness of life. These may be considered the general pattern, the archetypal. When we think of a dwelling, certain requirements are present—a roof and other protections from the environment, an entrance, eating space, sleeping space, as well as geographical location, nearness to necessary supplies such as water and food, etc. And there is an individual expression which is local and responsive to the uniqueness of the setting in which the language or the building is created and used. The personality, taste, vision and imagination of the individual builder are engaged to contribute to the idiosyncratic manifestation of the collective pattern.

The house (Indo-European root *dh-mo*, related to "making, doing, dwelling") is given life by its intimate connection with the community. The production and reproduction of the houses and buildings, all of the structures of the family and community, express the community. The house is for the family and is the family.

The nomad, the artist, the captain of industry, the accountant and the shopkeeper gather with their familiars at dusk under some canopy propped to mark a human sky, one under which man need not feel his shameless limits before God. He joins with his loved ones and sleeps his requisite hours in warmth and shelter. No man wishes to lie naked and alone in the field in the night blizzard. All are fathers when they pitch the tent or pour the foundation, since they structure a place discerned from nature.

Homelessness is dreadful. The homeless one is also fatherless. He has no guide, no protector, no *dh-mo*, no being. For some, for those whose terrestrial father is chaotic, loveless, incapable of constructing, their fate may be to roam the land naked and bereaved, sick in spirit and soma.

The homeless have no father, no roof, no house. These human beings are viewed as vermin by those who bloodlessly pose as fathers in our country—lawmakers. Yet the father is only as strong as his family. Yet we who are children or wives of these fathers of our country could cry out to them that the house is fatherless, weak, paltry, torn when our brothers and sisters live in shame, violence and terror. Albert Schweitzer wrote that the first and most fundamental right of man is the "right to habitation." A good father finds a place for his family.

This point—making "home" and "dwelling in it"—is

taken up by Philip Rawson in an essay on art—specifically ceramics—and function. His question concerns the creating of objects, the experience of their presence in the world and our relationship to them in terms of their reference to both fundamental patterns of our heritage and to the idiosyncrasy of the individual. He frequently refers to Heidegger, a philosopher whose persistent theme is the relationship of the immediate physical world and Being. Rawson writes, "Our problem Heidegger identified as that of finding our way 'home,' not by denying our heritage, but by carrying it with us as we must; we need somehow to incorporate it into a different order of *dasein*, overcoming the alienation between mankind and world which our heritage has engendered" (1985, p. 10).

The experience of a proper relationship to pattern, to those fundamental images from our "home," is what I am calling "fathering" here, the building of an approach which recognizes the guiding patriarchal structure and the immediacy of the "environment" in which the building or making is taking place. To quote Rawson further,

> It is more than probable that much of our current doubt about the aesthetics of function springs from our recent obsessions with endless experiment without any particular ultimate image in mind. Such an image cannot just remain a general look or effect. Effects can be lies. The sheer visibility of work-process as play is no guarantee of truth. What does guarantee it is the matching of conceptual integrity with feeling, of challenging and stretching coherent grammar and syntax by genuine intuited meaning. (Ibid., p. 11)

Repair

A house we all inhabit is language. Words and thought have
fallen into disrepute in recent scabrous decades. The vestiges
in which we still dwell are slovenly and rancid. Man voids
in his own stall the day long, never noticing his words nor
his thoughts and then lies down in filth at nightfall. Language
now is stenchy; smell your magazine emporiums, book stalls,
the unhappy scribbles of government documents, 'business
communiqués' (sad ironical term), the heaps of immemo-
rable memoranda. The craft of Homer has fallen to dust.
No joint fits or clasps beautifully to another in buildings or
in our messages to each other. Many of us no longer write
letters, and the ephemeral telephone can carry sad ejacula-
tions at 186,000 miles per second.

Jorge Luis Borges spoke of an image central to him and
to many writers when he said in an interview, "I always
thought of paradise as a library" (Barnstone, p. 149). The
basic mysteries of existence, time, friendship, death, horror,
the monstrous and the beautiful are addressed, befriended
and known through literature, through the pleasure of
reading. Again, Borges: "One should think of reading as a
form of happiness, as a form of joy. I think of compulsory
reading as wrong. You might as well speak of compulsory
love or compulsory happiness. One should read for the
pleasure of the book" (Barnstone, p. 113). Borges's own joys
encompass a number of writers and their works, notably *The
1001 Arabian Nights,* the work of Whitman, Poe, Emerson,
Stevenson, De Quincey and Robert Frost.

Borges, speaking of lines of Frost's poem "Acquainted
with the Night," and of other work of Frost's, names the chief

achievement of this poet that "he could write poems that seemed simple. But everytime you read them you are delving deeper and finding many winding paths and many different senses. So Frost has given us a new idea of metaphor. He gives us metaphor in such a way that we take it as a simple, straightforward statement" (Barnstone, p. 149).

The houses of literature, the novel, the poem—especially forms of the poem such as the sonnet—in order to carry their special design, request a particular form: dramatic form, the development of plot, the rhymes of language, alliteration, meter, so that, when Yeats writes of the "dolphin torn, gong tormented sea," he fashions from the same material as Homer, who tells of the "rose-fingered dawn." The forms of literature are not forms arbitrarily assigned. They are forms which have arisen from the character of human experience. Telling events in a long story, condensing experience in a metaphor, understanding that develops in a dialogue or conversation, the contradictions and impossibilities when we tell a nightmare—these are all patterns given to each human being, the gift of the house of language, the father's house.

Telling the story of our experience to others is a form of integrity, a form of crafting our being and our connection with other people. When we tell stories to each other, we form ourselves and our community with others. The care with which we tell the story demonstrates the care which we have for ourselves and for other people. Joseph Breuer's term for psychotherapy is "the talking cure." Mere talking, however, is not a repair in itself, though it can provide an opportunity for one. When we choose an image or a story or a way of speaking which reflects our sense of integrity, we offer a repair to ourselves and others.

A well-crafted house, built with care and thoughtfulness, invites others to visit. Speaking mindfully, with consideration for one's own integrity and that of others, built in a place and in such a manner that respects the land, invites others to join us. A father knows his house reflects his person. A well-tended house in good repair invites the inner man and the outer man to companionship.

When integrity and feeling do not match or have not come to a synthesis in the process of building, structural cohesion may be missing. This is as true in the rule of the family, the relationships of people and their language, metaphors, feelings and thoughts as it is in the actual construction of buildings, since both groups of processes refer to Being.

A well-designed, well-built cabin artfully and respectfully placed by a freestone river with a reach of peaks in view and trout rising in a long pool transforms the location from a place of wild, unconscious geological processes to one of beauty perceived, an image of Being and Dwelling, a home in Being. On the other hand, a house or structure poorly designed and built of chaff, awkwardly and thoughtlessly thrown up by drug-intoxicated builders, violates the earth and creates bad fathering. A house or building which is lifeless and chaotic, rude and abrasive leaves its family fatherless, impoverished, anxious and directionless. When such links between humanity and the world are not observed, when those who have eyes to see and minds to read do not join Being and Doing, there is a break, a suffering and a destruction, an "endless experiment without any particular image in mind." When such disruption is at hand, it calls for a response, for what I call here a Repair.

Alas, the American fantasy of true wilderness is, today,

a delusion. There are too many people who wish—rightfully so—to flee the ugly and artless suburbs they inhabit and encounter the robust aesthetics of wild nature. A more realistic policy is a well-fathered 'preserve'—areas where wildness may continue, the slow patterning of the natural world, ringed by homes crafted with a measured pace. Some forest, some land must fall to the dozer and the blade of civilization in order that any land—its foxes, elk, bear and wolverine—be saved. Oddly enough, the spontaneous vigor of a forest today depends more on the regulation of the patriarch than ever before. The wood fire, once thought to be the very symbol of the free and natural home, is shown to be a bad offender to atmospheric pollution in ratio of use.

Father is an artfully made construction. How sad we become with no fathers. Those fathers of thought, such as Herodotus in history, Hippocrates in medicine, Aristotle and Socrates in philosophy, Sun Tzu in the art of war—how painstakingly and lovingly they joined thought to thought with resolute care and precision and aesthetic dexterity.

Art, literature, music, architecture, like our psychological and social structures, are in shambles for lack of decent fathering. Endless experiment—the hallmark of our century—is bankruptcy: nothing left in the account. And yet artists wonder why the government further limits grants. The attempt to create a particular effect, a gesture, a noise winds us into the void. Experimentation without house (*dh-mo*), family or father has no integrity, no endurance; it is a forlorn shade in Hades. Aesthetics, despite current argument, is not a matter of doubt. Beauty is quite simply the order, the rule, the fathering principle in nature joined with the mothering principle in nature—that is to say, form and content. Art which does not adore nature and the Gods is null, a vapor.

Describing the present state of dissolution of myth and religion, Joseph Campbell speaks of a breakdown in "monadic" structures or single-focused, single-minded perspectives. Campbell writes, "For there are no more intact monadic horizons: all are dissolving. And along with them, the psychological hold is weakening of the mythological images and related social rituals by which they were supported." And then he comments that

> The old gods are dead, or dying, and people everywhere are searching, asking: What is the new mythology to be, the mythology of this unified earth as of one harmonious being? . . . One cannot predict the next mythology any more than one can predict tonight's dream; for a mythology is not an ideology. (Pp. 116–17)

This is a description of Saturn-Kronos in his destructive aspect: ". . . prisoner or bondsman in . . . Tartarus . . . the god of death and the dead. . . . the devourer of children, eater of raw flesh, the consumer of all" (Hillman, 1979, p. 16).

When the archetypal pattern of integrity and genuine intuited meaning (Rawson) are not joined and there is dissolution, decay, consumption and sterility—the "monadic horizon" does not seem to serve—we see the negative aspect of Saturn-Kronos among us. This does not mean that Saturn-Kronos as a pattern of father should be annihilated. We cannot destroy the pattern of the father structure in any case, and attempts to eradicate Saturn-Kronos result in his negative aspect moving into the unconscious, not disappearing.

What may be practiced is a simultaneous awareness of the bipolar aspect of Saturn-Kronos, a Repair. This is an image with rich connotations and possibilities. There are two verbs "to repair" in English with different meanings and different etymologies; yet they are related, as we will see, and both very useful in the present discussion.

The first "repair" we look at signifies, according to *Webster's New World Dictionary,* "(1) to put back in good condition after damage, decay, etc.; mend; fix, (2) to renew; restore; revive; as, repair one's health, (3) to amend; set right; remedy; as repair the mistake, (4) to make amends for; make up for; compensate."

The word "repair" arises from Latin *re* plus *parare,* "to get, prepare, make ready"; and from Indo-European *per,* "to bring forward, bring forth," as in various images which refer to young animals, such as German *Farre,* "bullock," Greek *portis,* "calf," Old Indian *prthukah,* "child, calf, young of an animal." Thus "repair" in this sense has to do with animal youthfulness being experienced or made over again—a kind of rebirth.

The image of renewal or rebirth has been used throughout cultural and religious traditions worldwide to describe a repair that the human animal may undergo to discover, "bring forward, bring forth" a new nature or his fundamental child nature. Jesus admonishes us to become as children again, and traditional initiation rites (cf. Mircea Eliade) are examples of the widespread use of the image of rebirth. When we are first born, there is more innocence in us, in the sense of willing and choosing, and less life experience than when we are reborn; when we "*reparare*," we must choose birth after "damage, decay," suffering. And, as pointed out by those who have studied initiation rituals, the *reparare* itself includes physical, emotional and spiritual suffering.

This sense of reconnection with the child, the making over again that we see in the first "repair," is also in the second "repair." This version is defined by *Webster's* as "(1) to go (to a place); to betake oneself, (2) to go often, customarily, or in numbers; as, they repaired daily to the park, (3) [Obs.], to return. And in an archaic noun sense, a place to which a person or persons go often or customarily; resort; haunt." The roots of this word are Latin *re* and *patria*, "country, homeland." Thus to repair in this sense is to unite oneself with the country of one's origin but, even more important for this discussion, to unite oneself again with the *patria* and the *patris*.

This image refers in part to one's father but more fundamentally to heritage, to pattern. This is what Rawson and Heidegger mean by ". . . finding our way 'home,' not by denying our heritage, but by carrying it with us as we must; we need somehow to incorporate it into a different order of *dasein*, overcoming the alienation between mankind and world which our heritage has engendered" (Rawson, 1985, p. 10). In this quote, we see that the heritage has engendered alienation—one side of Saturn-Kronos—and also is what we must incorporate, make physical and experience—the other side of Saturn-Kronos. Both the creation and the destruction are important to keep in awareness. To see again—to experience without denying either aspect—the "bipolar" quality of Saturn-Kronos is a healing repair in this sense of the word.

The two poles of the Saturn-Kronos figure, the builder,

creator, maintainer on the one hand and the sterile, detached destroyer on the other, may seem quite far apart, but they are both necessary in any conjunction of Being and *dasein*, any creative act; they are inseparable in our actions and even in the foundation of our actions. In simpler language, it may be said that *as the father marks us, so we mark the world.* Aristotle maintained that it was the male seed which was the active and procreative agent and the womb of woman the recipient of this seed: "Plowing and sowing were conceived in almost all Indo-European languages as symbolic for the male, while the 'furrow' was associated with the female" (Thass-Thienemann, p. 285). Yet to take this symbolic representation literally—as admittedly most cultures have in historic memory—is to miss the *patris as symbol* (as pattern) and thus to miss the rich possibilities of symbolic repair that may arise in the joining of the aspects of the *patris.*

Any careful reading of biology or observation of the life processes in man or animal will yield the awareness that death is part of life and that men and women both are capable of and demonstrate attitudes and actions which are creative and destructive, which reveal both sides of Saturn-Kronos. Women are as capable of devouring their children—perhaps more so—than men. We only need remember the Greek Medea to understand this.

Medea was a niece of Circe, the great witch, and a priestess of Hecate. Her reputation as a witch even surpassed that of Circe. When Jason came to Caucis on his quest for the Golden Fleece, Medea aided him out of her love for him. Through potions, spells and cunning, she helped the Argonauts in several adventures, such as mesmerizing the Cretan monster Talos by using an evil eye. However, when Jason abandoned her for Glauce, Medea sent Glauce a poison garment which burned her alive, burned the royal family she was a part of and the palace itself. Afterward, she turned to her own children by Jason and savagely eviscerated them.

We may also call on Kali, the terrible aspect of the Devi or Mahadevi, the mother-goddess consort of Shiva. She has two main aspects: a "mild" one, represented by four primary qualities and with the images of jewels, food and the beautiful; and a "terrible" aspect, represented by Chandi, Daevi, Durga and Kali. Fierce, terrible, inaccessible, black, Kali is shown as hideous; her emblems are the noose, the iron hook and a rosary of skulls. She is sometimes pictured as a voracious hag feeding on the entrails of human beings, standing in a boat on an ocean of blood, drinking the life blood from the skulls of children. In her two right hands she holds knives for severing the life from her victims. In her left hands she holds a bowl of food and a lotus. She symbolizes the life force, giving and taking away, the creating and consuming power of the Goddess.

Dread, necessity, temporality and/or our own finitude are experiences which, far from only limiting us, actually are in large measure impulses to our creativity. Heidegger writes, "The call comes *from me* and yet *from beyond me*" (p. 320).

The great Scottish poet Hugh MacDiarmid vividly portrays the relationship between the poles of Kronos and how this relationship is enacted in inspiration which comes *from me* and *from beyond me* in his poem "The Salmon Leap":

> I saw one shadow shoot up and over
> While ten failed to make it again and again,
> But most of the salmon without an effort
> In the bottom of the pool all day had lain.

> Suddenly, effortlessly, like a flight of birds,
> Up and over I saw them all slip.
> The secret, I think, was the melted snow
> Coming down and flicking them like a whip.
>
> The majority of people make no attempt
> In life to explore the infinite.
> But who can tell what Death's cold touch
> May prompt the lazy louts to yet?
>
> (P. 553)

The natural desire of the salmon to return "home," follow and realize the structure of their pattern is an expression of repair. The desire to repair seems not to be sufficient in itself, however; MacDiarmid expresses his view that the "secret" is the cold melted snow "coming down and flicking [the salmon] . . . like a whip."

The call *from me* and *from beyond me* is portrayed in the desire to return home innate in the salmon and in man. That is, all being returns to death and spiritual reality, and the call to do so is forever present and mighty in the tissue and psyche.

In the poem, a lone shadow, dark, singular, a warrior alone, shoots up and over, suggesting an otherworldly figure who goes on beyond others in a unique burst—perhaps Amidha Buddha or a Fish such as Jesus—who ascends and transcends in particularity. It is tempting to suggest this figure is Jung's 'individuated man', he who has integrated the rejected aspect of his nature (the shadow) and gained a connection between the corporeal earth and the transcendent world of spirit; he moves freely and naturally between worlds.

Ten others try and fail. Their failure perhaps suggests those who have heard some of the call within and the call from beyond but are wedged in a world of 'effort.' These figures relentlessly attempt—we may say with will and conscious struggle—to 'achieve goals.' The shadow doesn't *try*, however; it simply *does*.

Meanwhile the drones merely subsist in the bottom of the pool. Or are they wiser than those who beat their bellies against the rock? Are they waiting patiently for the moment of the call "from beyond" to move?

MacDiarmid figures them as primarily unconscious 'louts,' as well one might, since they live reactively and in the glum noiselessness of the river pool's sleepy and blanketed bed. They have come thus far through mere instinct. As a cocoon of peace and timelessness, the lulling pool is fine for them. Yet this cove of listlessness is delusion, since all must go 'up and over.' They wobble their gills in herdish, suburban dawdling.

What finally whips them all into ascent is, ironically, the cold. Even the louts now move and rise above; this demonstrates that higher purpose may yet pull us to repair even if we must be flicked and whipped.

Truth is cold, and the glacial dread of our own finiteness contains the bitterest truths. Yet in human history is it not the eras of greatest threat of apocalypse which have whipped us to spiritual exploration? Our own age, with its holocausts and criminal horrors, terrorists, sexual aberrations, religious corruption, all manner of malignity in families, and the goriest and most evil weaponry ever in the grasp of the very recently evolved opposable thumb and forefinger of man— this age has spawned the juiciest harvest of spiritual delicacies available in the millennium, from the elegant and frigid 'demythologization' of Christianity of Rudolf Bultmann and his pals through the revivals of spiritism, theosophy, and astrology, the rediscovery of mystics of various epochs, the explosion of Christian and neo-Christian sects, the various cultic movements, the 'psychologization' of religion and mythology, and the multiple 'meetings of East and West,' chanting and channeling and glossolalia. From the glinting, ghastly brains of scientists who spawned the bomb have come repentant and doleful predictions of nuclear winter—a frozen, immobile world still and static for a million years.

> But who can tell what Death's cold touch
> May prompt the lazy louts to yet?

The patriarch, in his figure of warmonger, destroyer, annihilator, is blamed for the bomb. Yet it was only after the bomb's birth that the grand, strong parade of social rights activism for women and ethnic groups began in earnest in America. The cold blade of reason spawned reason and unreason. The bomb resembles, more than any other anatomical image, mother's womb; the bomb is a mother, a mother-devourer, a fatal cradle. She is Macha, Celtic Goddess of war, who feeds on the heads of men killed in battle. The devouring Macha, the bomb mother, is prepared to consume her babies, as is Saturn-Kronos, the primordial father, who devours his own children.

The child of the nuclear age can become a product of the sperm of hatred and the atomic womb. He can become a source for mutual blaming, a receptacle for the violence and maliciousness of his parents. The innocence of those newly born can be a vessel for the bile of those charged with nuclear hatred. This is being graphically and concretely experienced by children raised in abusive, violent, splintered homes—perhaps by now more of a norm than an aberration. In extreme situations, children are ritually abused, sexually tortured in unspeakable manners, forced to kill their beloved pets—even forced to murder other children or babies. One might hope that such extreme forms were rare, but evidence is beginning to accumulate that they are possibly not so unusual.

The "average" children, meanwhile, are routinely, incessantly exposed by movies, videotapes and music lyrics to violence, sadism, pornography, brutality; they are given no vessel in which to contain such imagery. The stories of Kali, of Medea, of Saturn, the sacrifices of the Aztecs, the cannibalistic practices of certain aborigines, the gory imagery of Papua New Guinea—all these had mythological and cultural containers within which they had meaning. When Saturn swallows his children, one of them, Zeus, frees his brothers and sisters. Kali, despite her ferocious, consuming aspect, her swords and skulls and blood, still brings forth children; she holds in her hand the lotus (symbol of great beauty) and provides nourishment for her children. She is known as the embodiment of both creation and destruction. This mix of elements communicates both despair and hope, creativity and possibility despite the limits of time and death. What can a boy do who listens to a song or views a videotape of an enormously financially successful rock group when it advocates rape, assault, anarchy, escape from the culture into violence, drugs, disrespect for family, the betrayal of friends? What of a culture of children brought up on *Nightmare on Elm Street*? Where is the father?

Father Warrior

Nature is often ungentle. All living things die and mostly in violence, victim to starvation, to more powerful creatures, to the hazards and inscrutable extremes of weather. Man, as the fiercest predator in nature, represents the greatest threat to the fair and balanced cruelty of the physical order of life, since his power can be multiplied so manifestly beyond the reach of his own musculo-skeletal limits, unlike any other breathing, pulsing mammal who can only kill what he can out-muscle or out-maneuver. And standing at the very pinnacle of male ungentleness is Kronos, the patriarch, willful and controlling. We read in the patriarchal text Genesis that God gave man dominion over the seas, the land and everything that crawls on the land, from which directive men and women built civilization, often with little regard for the fragility or mortality of living beings.

The forebears of civilization are the warriors and the Gods of war, who are also the Gods of order in the cosmos. Creation may only be maintained through the circle of destruction and regeneration. Mars incarnates this dual aspect. He is figured with a sword, but the blade apparently furrows as well, since the farmers of the Mediterranean appealed to him for good harvests.

A third aspect of Mars, combining the symbols of war and agriculture, is dance. Mars was trained early by the centaurs as a dancer. Swords and planting sticks are joined in the dancer's hand in battle mime and to celebrate victory in battle and preparation for war. Festivities of Mars as warrior took place in March. His agricultural aspect was honored in May. He is God of spring.

Rending veins and the flow of blood have always eloquently represented the appearance of new life bursting, the flow of rivers, time and the Turn of the Wheel of the Year. Titans well may devour the sun and swallow the clouds without the intervention of warriors; more practically, no one wishes to wake at night to the cold blade of the aborigine slitting the family's throats and plundering the crops. The icy natural law called for a death for each life, however, and therefore a drawing of edges of division, strife, conflict, suffering, death.

When Jesus says I died so that you may live, his words are quite unoriginal, having endured millennia of Semitic tradition. War is the natural state of homeostasis in all corporeal being. Whether this is shameful or superb we do not know; yet the fact remains. Transcendence, really, is only a matter for when the coals of the prepuce are cold ashes. We ought, I suppose, to seek some forms of transcorporeal bliss, but man is stupid and burns and cannot.

And he does burn; so the burning and his clashes and battles and venery and speculation are his bliss. This is what the father has known and taught in every culture till now. And now the father warrior has new challenges. He must teach, and another of the infinite series of new ages and new questions unfolds.

The father warrior has to strike out again with the help of Mars to fuse the unformed world of the potential—the future—with the materialized and now rotting present. Some form of bloodshed and war is demanded by human tissue, whether generalized by the burning scourge of nuclear incendiation, a raft of small wars, or simply the self-annihilation and homeostasis represented by fatal drug consumption, AIDS or domestic violence. Perhaps there are other forms less deadly. Certainly recent art has sought to prism and bottle pain and violence; yet it has remained abstract. Perhaps violent varieties of modern music are a vessel for the pulsation of tissue. Some embodiment of the warrior inhabits the tissue and would best be cultivated, known, received, so that our heritage, our immanent dowry be respected.

The wars rage, the battles continue, the great hunt goes on and Odysseus remains wandering in the inner man. He continues to plow fields deep in the psyche; he continues to rage and burn. The seasons of weather cycle in his being. Cain slays Abel every day of the earth. Proper work for the father warrior is work infused with and undertaken in risk. To wander with Odysseus and battle and challenge. The fields he plows and the fields upon which he battles take many forms. No single occupation defines the father warrior. Rather, it is a perspective, a sensibility and a commitment.

In academia, he challenges the assumptions of his field and battles for knowledge which is ethical and meaningful and contributes to his personal life, the life of his family and that of his community. In retail work he chooses and presents his products with an eye to their effects beyond his store window: the environmental impact of the products, the political implications of their manufacture and their influence in the lives of his brother consumers.

The artist presents artwork whose form, materials and content challenge current meaning and taste, while maintaining a deep respect for its origins, for history and for the art viewer's integrity. The most powerful weapons of the artist warrior are discipline and love: the consummate mastery of craft and the desire to bind people together in the experience of beauty. The artist serves Eros.

The business executive as father warrior understands

that corporations are machines of war and that implications of every transaction he makes are international, political and are written in blood—his own and those of the people he loves and hates. The carpenter, the mechanic, the artisan take risks at great odds and at great cost to themselves, using the finest materials and the highest workmanship, with the realization that this is an act of terrorism and a threat to the well-being of an unconscious society. The scientist boldly takes his place as the priest of his age. He reports his successes and failures with the understanding that both are impossible statements and with the full realization that his concept of the truth will, in the twinkling of an eye, be considered superstition and fallacy. The journalist reports his sense of the truth by day and expiates his shame as a liar by night. The doctor intervenes in the body as a last resort, rather than as a simple solution, and carefully considers the literature which demonstrates the violence of his art. When he cuts, he cuts well, directly and without hesitation. The risk undertaken by the therapist is to embrace his puny understanding of the psyche, yet to view the profession of shaman as a high calling demanding lifelong attention to his own failings. The father warrior as policeman undertakes the arduous task of compassion for perpetrators and risks perpetration himself.

Proper work is war. In the inner man, it is most vigorous battle, requiring honesty of the most brutal sort. The crux of this honesty is to do and choose what he grasps as best and right and proper with respectful awareness that he is wrong. Martin Luther has said it best: *peca fortitis,* "sin boldly." The warrior is the person who presents and opens himself to the richness of life as it is and "goes to war" for what he believes to be right, honest, true.

The father warrior embodies a reconciliation of conflicting tendencies, arising from his fundamental Saturnian opposites, the urge to build and the urge to consume. His qualities are forbearance and vigor, force and serenity, yearning and dispassion, rectitude and craftiness, volition and devotion, grit, integrity and clemency. His polestar is Homer's Odysseus, who incarnates also self-knowledge, courage, doubt and skill, who does not shrink from threat or potential harm, yet who neither seeks nor loves violence in itself.

Forbearance, Vigor

Odysseus, King of Ithaca, is lost returning from the siege of Troy and wanders for ten years seeking his home. Father, mired in the groaning, travailing world, suffers Odysseus's homesickness, his yearning for *dh-mo*, for the place and center of being, the *patria*, for his wife, his son, his land. Yet the riotous, luxuriant world thrills him.

Odysseus adventures at sea, roiled by the rage of Poseidon, caught in another primordial form of father— Poseidon's fury toward Odysseus's arrogance and daring. He wanders to the isles of Cyclops, to Circe's ingle, to the side of treacherous Calypso, among the Phaecians and to sundry other wonders and perils. Odysseus longs to arrive at his bed, where his wife Penelope aches and burns and withstands usurpers to the throne. Ithaca is all in anarchy. Telemachos, his son, needs his father. Yet though Odysseus ails of distance and bewilderment, victim of nature and Gods, he does not collapse but strives, losing good men to monsters, losing ships and nearly losing hope or dear life himself. And he goes on with vigor, striding and sailing into destiny, carrying also with him terror and longing, the possibility of never returning home and the heaviness of grief in his distance from his family.

The father warrior puts himself on the line in the endeavors of life. He responds to the 'call' which comes from him and from beyond him. As a man in combat, father today—in the office, the plant, the emporium, in the mill or on the chär—labors estranged from his *dh-mo;* and he has urgent need of Odysseus's forbearance and drive to spell and buoy his homesickness. Work today is perhaps furthest ever from the heart, since the factotum and the executive alike grind under technology as unbridled as the hungry mouth of Cyclops devouring good men. Father needs now in no less measure than Odysseus a forbearing vigorous hope for home to be reached through perseverance. What man feels at home? Yet he must seek it and meanwhile live in a richness which, though it is not home, is loamy and exuberant.

Force, Serenity

Force is masculine—phallic—and holds a mystery of feminine fluidity. This is the inspiring aspect of the anima, encouraging masculinity. Serenity is cloudless, clear and fair. Odysseus can roam the watery world seeking his being and guarding home in a well-held memory of dry, clear Ithaca. Penelope waits in a more sodden, dank and muddy land than Odysseus can know, however—but her heart stays fair though her eyes tear. The Old Indian word for "serene" means "to burn," as the sun burns clouds. Serenity then can clear obscurity. Odysseus needs a rarefied image of Ithaca, Penelope and Telemachos, a clarity at the center, to fuel his force, to drive the fluid of muscles and to advance on the sea.

If Penelope today will not wait but lies down with the

first bleating ram who crosses her field, Father's force withers and he cannot return home. Penelope today has discovered that she need not wait. Why should she endure a husband's absence while he snorkels the wide world? No reason to her can defend waiting; rather, reason suggests in our time Penelope's packing forth and good riddance to the bastard himself. This is just, but were she to stay put a bit longer than fashion asks, he would return to where he longs to be— with his *familia y esposa.* Ten years is a terrible endurance, but the father warrior wanders that long or longer, sometimes, lost. Men hanker after corporate advancement, and it takes ten years or more to climb the ladder and step off into the chasm of self-doubt.

Such absence, as Homer shows, is constitutive of the man who receives the crown of force, that is, the man who is indeed a son and king of Ithaca, as all good fathers are. When he returns from his wanderings—perhaps in the rolling vagaries of business, industry or the intellectual life—he will be a man true and tested by experience, fully empowered and present to life. Yet also he returns in wonder and marveling, having seen the impossible lands. Like "Boots," he comes to power through "wondering and wandering."

Our new Penelope often prefers an attentive mate who dotes on her moments, in many cases a poltroon who sings high. Rightfully so, however, since the father warrior so often goes frail, miserable, detached, feckless and prostrates himself, wailing in anxiety, forgetting his wondering, his journey, his discovery of monsters, sirens, strange lands. He settles into dullness. The father who wobbles and surrenders his vision of home and his force relinquishes his serenity. What Penelope can expect his ship to come to harbor? The renewal of his vision of return to Penelope and Telemachos—while being drawn to the wonders of the Sirens, of beautiful Goddesses and enchanting isles—is what draws him home.

The exercise of force, when not connected with serenity, does not lead home. Edward Dahlberg points out that man is the only one among animals who voids in his own house; the father warrior does not destroy his house and family by wholesale pillage and destruction of the watery world. Destruction of nature is also harm of his own being. He does not eliminate forest; he prunes it. He does not urinate in his drinking cup; therefore neither does he heave garbage into the river. The serenity of wife, home and son is what he wants, not frowsy, slutty consort.

Rectitude, Craftiness

The work of the father warrior is well and honestly done. He does not lie to his son but truthfully reports his failures (unlike the ignoble American leadership in the gory futility referred to as the Vietnam Conflict). He speaks and acts directly, though he may be named a fool. He doubts, grieves and laments in season. He does not hit children or women, though he recognizes the impulse as human.

Rectitude is the fine-tuning of restraint and unleashing of power when necessary. Display of force for self-aggrandizement, though nearly the industry standard in our poor age, is unthinkable to the father warrior. He practices bloodsport with reserve and humility, employing technology only to reduce his advantage, kills a minimal bag in hunting and releases all but an infrequent brace of fish, the few which he carves and eats to salubriously remind him of his barbarity, his inescapable animal tissue, and to think as the fish does.

Rectitude clearly does not exclude skill, craft, cunning, expertise. Craftiness, that ability to generate effects through imagination, is a quality of value for the father warrior. Craftiness may be discriminated from treachery, malicious deceit and insidiousness. This is a distinction not often made in the haggling, dickering affairs of merchantry and 'human service,' and because of this confusion so many negotiations descend into the entanglements of law courts, hospitals and morgues.

One must add, however, that these latter are worlds in themselves of great interest and richness, and if one finds oneself in them, as Odysseus found himself in various isles of treachery and peril, one may do well to directly enter their vileness and bottomless imagery. Indeed, this is an aspect of the quality of craftiness, that is, the ability to enter the unavoidable suffering of the world, endure it and transmute it into meaning; to exercise skill, horse sense and timing to gather whatever fruition may be available at the time; to be instructed and guided by the Gods of the event and to use sufficient means for protection for oneself and one's family.

The soul delights in imagery and has its life in variety. Darkness, peril, homicidal and suicidal treachery, the so-called "pathological side of life"—we know now that these are part of the natural spectrum of the soul's fantasy and have an important place in our full experience of psyche. Acceptance of our own and others' "tendencies" to such pathologies increases compassion and understanding and frees us of the compulsion to act. Confession of a desire to harm another depotentiates the urge, since the act is experienced in confessing it to oneself and to others. Eros is present in the revelation of our guile to others, binding us to them with cords from heart chakra to heart chakra. Energy then is bound and flowing within community and fellowship.

The father warrior knows the gimcrack hungers of his compatriots. He knows how to produce bread from dust like any good 'picaro,' how to elude a fight in which he will only fall under the boots of a thug and how to harvest life and coins from a moment of apparent pitfalls.

He wanders the boundless and pitiless earth raw and acrimonious—now afraid and near naked like Cain, now dressed in proper attire, now in anile or androgynous garments—and conducts himself at times with virtue and good sense, self-irony, imagination and the certainty that the affairs of mankind are, after all, a sorry and murky and mean attempt to reflect the eternal lights of the Transcendent One. Cain is crafty and marked by God for guile, envy and murder and to wander widely. Odysseus, knowing the use of androgynous garments, sought Achilles in the women's quarters and thus began his wanderings.

Father warrior embodies these traits of mutability, change and new possibilities. And he employs his skills for the safeguarding of the house. Having set the planks and reeds, stretched the skins, mortared the quarried rock, will he now be a ninny and let the first rascal who knocks on the door take possession of his wife and *dh-mo*? So, another element of craftiness is protection of one's goods through imaginative effort, not through malice but through cunning.

Cunning requires thorough knowledge of the hungers of one's age. Does the herd lust for rare goods, unusual pleasures, exquisite raiment, plush conveyances? Alternately, does the time call for monastic simplicity, sackcloth and uncomfortable seating to inspire humility? The father warrior knows how to provide for his times.

At the same time the Father Warrior is crafty, he is in some measure gullible, since he is curious, searching and venturesome. We might consider the well-known American figure who eternally suffers the consequences of curiosity, ardency, haste and recklessness—Coyote. Coyote is the balance weight to rectitude in the father warrior, the hidden and necessary equipoise to a probity tempted by piety or self-righteousness. Inventive, hungry, sexually vigorous and supple, quick-minded, opportunistic, Coyote is a vibrant and dynamic figure but one who often finds himself in hot broths as a result of his own misattentions.

Coyote meets trouble partly as a result of his curiosity and partly from his hungers. In a Hopi story, Coyote volunteers to take an offering to the Grand Canyon to pray for rain for the people at Orayvi but forgets his mission when he sees a naked girl swimming in a spring. Naked girls are most irresistible to Coyote. His lechery is documented widely in Hopi and other stories, as are his impatience and capriciousness. In another story, Coyote is helping Spider Woman distribute stars in the sky. At first he arranges them carefully but soon tires of the painstaking work and tosses the rest, scattering them as they are now, across the sky. Another time, he tries to bring fire to man but catches his pelt on fire.

Coyote cannot resist food, even when he suspects a trap; nor the temptation to find out what is over the next hill, even when he may miss a chance to catch something for dinner for his starving family; nor the opportunity to play a trick on another, though his efforts often backfire. Such efforts often result in his own death, since everyone knows he can be duped and that his resistance to temptation is quite small. He can never refuse a beautiful girl. One name for Coyote in Hopi is *lowason'isaw,* which means "cunt-craving Coyote."

The drives of nature, the lure of gratification and inquisitiveness are his bane but also attributes of his lively and animated
character.

The craftiness and guile of Coyote are equal to rectitude
as aspects of the good patriarch. The meaning of the wanderings of Odysseus is carried in his kingship, the rightness of
his claim to fatherhood and sovereignty in his land, and in
his wiliness, his cunning, his hunger, his visceral excitement.
The good *pater,* a father of integrity, honors and respects the
call to righteousness, certainty and kingship, as well as his
Coyote-nature, his hungers, his desires, his longings.

Wandering the world, the warrior encounters seduc-
tions—kingship and power and the satisfactions of his desires. He could sell drugs; there is a secretary at the office;
he is alone with the babysitter; he could have a promotion,
if; the Sunday School needs a teacher; "why don't you leave
what you are doing and get a real job?" Recognizing his
Coyote-nature, he considers the possibilities.

A story is told among some cultures that snakes approach their victims while these are asleep. Then they enter
through the rectum, biting and poisoning the bowels, killing the victim. Rectitude, righteousness and piety, without
proper attention to the snake nature, create itchy longings,
fouled bowels, colitis, ulcers, diarrhea.

Integrity

Integrity, for the father warrior who lives, breathes and
dreams in the world, is a matter of multiplicity. Integrity is
often taken to mean blamelessness, purity and uprightness,
in the sense of a clean, righteous, phariseeistic thought and
action. This standard diminishes and restricts human experience and, if integrity can mean "whole or complete"

(Latin *integritas*), surely makes the full richness of human existence beyond our reach.

The word "integrity" derives from Latin *integer*, meaning "undiminished, unhurt, unimpaired," and from *in* plus *tangere*, meaning "untouched." The man of integrity, then, is undiminished; he encircles body, mind and soul and does not condemn or banish any of them, nor does he live for one over another. To live only for one or another aspect of his being is impairment and reduction of himself and an over-personalization of his experience. The phrase in Matthew, "man does not live by bread alone," is not meant to suggest that bread—that is, the body—is unimportant; rather, it suggests multiplicity and variety in living.

Grit

At the same time he engages and wrestles circumstances, the father warrior maintains a kernel of cool sempiternity in his gut. The word "grit" refers to coarse grain or a kernel, a dense impersonal nugget which here refers to the enduring authority the father warrior feels inside but does not attribute to himself. In this sense he is *in-tangere*, untouched, because he does not personalize events but rather moves with them. Thus he does not avoid life through detachment—a perspective which takes life too negatively and personalizes the ordinary flow of experience and wishes to annihilate experience—nor does he take the occurrences of material life as an end in themselves. Father warrior is *lowason'isaw*—"cunt-craving Coyote"—and *spiritus rector*—spiritual father.

Volition, Ambition and Devotion

Volition is the act of willing, that is, the exercise of wish, choice, hope, preference for a perceived good. What Freud calls *das ich,* the 'I' (ego), seeks satisfaction and enchantment for the living creature through ambition, the maximizing of the flow of chosen goods to one's house. Volition binds the father warrior to the world. The God of this binding is Eros, who fastens man to earth, draws him to mingle with his tribe and inspires him to build his house, his friendships and his name.

Etymologically, the word "ambition" means "to go around," as politicians go round canvassing support before an election. The father warrior goes round in the whirling sphere of the earth and men's affairs seeking a home, a clan and his own being. Unlike the solitary mercenary who craves conflict and gain for self-inflation, the father warrior goes round for support in bearing the load of the community. He seeks to devote himself to his family and his tribe. The vow of the father—made to Hestia or other hearth deities—is to be the house and to build from his tissue what construction he may. Thus his ambition goes round and encircles those to whom he is bound, his family, friends, tribe. What positive consequences fall from volition—from his ambition to unfold his own wishes and hopes and those of the people near him—he gives over freely to his people. This is his devotion.

The bhikku, the spiritual pilgrim, throws off the webbing of the world and seeks his freedom through devotion to his home in formlessness. The father warrior embraces the ten thousand things and worships form, though he knows that the fabric of the world is a shifting phantasm. He holds a reverential attitude to the integrity of the biological surgings and embodiments. He does not diminish what lives by calling phenomena 'nothing,' nor does he consider his volition final. He walks gently along the riverbank and builds a highway boldly but with shame.

Clemency

"Shame" means covering up one's nakedness, as Adam did. When we tear at the earth, slash her lovely flesh and build our own often hideous structures, we lay bare our infamy. Whereas it need not be a matter for remorse for the father to build for the community, he corrupts himself, his family and his tribe when he frays the land without reverence and then hastily constructs ill-conceived, shoddy edifices with cheap and temporary materials. This is unmanly, unfatherly, depraved, puerile.

The father warrior constructs his acts and his house with clemency, not with ruthlessness. Despite his great force, he is mild and indulgent. "Clemency" arises from the Greek word *klehemonos,* "inclined." The father warrior doesn't annihilate his surroundings but leans gently and firmly against the stones, trees and his fellows. He is disposed favorably to others and fashions his house to invite them. He builds on firm, well-secured ground, protected from howling winds, preferably on a mild slope, near a river or a friendly street.

He conducts himself with clemency for his family and his peers and remains at their side without complaint.

When attacked, he defends himself with whatever means demanded. If forced to kill another in defense, he does not hesitate but accomplishes the act, not dwelling on or delighting in his force. If he is criticized and admonished—here I rephrase what Gurdjieff's father told him—he listens carefully and ponders the opprobrium. If he finds that the critic is accurate, he thanks him and seeks the means of transformation. If he finds the attack slanderous and false, he does not respond if it concerns his conscience only but reacts with all available force if the attack involves his family or his tribe and may wound them.

He does not demand that others think, feel or see as he does but employs reason, persuasion and imagination—not deceit—to alter their judgment.

And as the true warrior responds to this call which speaks of a necessity, an integrity and an inevitability he accepts, so too does the true builder carry out his making with risk, with a sense of his abilities and limitations. An aesthetic value works like MacDiarmid's "whip" to the maker or builder who creates the *dh-mo,* the house, as his response to his being and in service to his family.

The architect and theorist Christopher Alexander and his colleagues develop in their many works the view that the making of dwellings, buildings, towns and cities involves—when done with integrity and authenticity—a response to ancient patterns and the deeply felt and considered idiosyncrasies of the individual. Such a way of building results in a timeless and aesthetically rich texture of human life which incorporates tension and harmony, personal will and self-abnegation, in the sense of seeing beyond cleverness.

The Female Patriarch

Though she has many times been given less recognition in the men's house than she may have deserved, the female patriarch has existed and may be an increasingly important figure in the shifting mythology of our time and the future.

Many images and metaphors arising from the historical and linguistic roots of the patriarch have been identified in this discussion. The *patris* figure (Saturn-Kronos) is definitely male and tied to the manifestation of traditionally masculine qualities. Yet, though these qualities are most syntonic with men and men traditionally have felt most closely allied with the patriarch, for various reasons they currently seem to be less willing to identify with the *patris,* with the rich possibilities offered by the patterns of their heritage. Stereotyped, wretched, cheap, unpleasant, uninviting, superficial and unaesthetic products, services and buildings are being offered thoughtlessly and without compassion in the post-industrial countries. Rather than warriors with forbearance and vigor, force and serenity, yearning and dispassion, rectitude and craftiness, grit, integrity and clemency, our current warrior images demonstrate self-indulgence, jitteriness, impatience, psychopathy, velocity and cosmetic cleverness. An evening of television will demonstrate this to even the casual viewer.

Have men forgotten and disavowed the *patris,* perhaps in a response to feminism and charges of insensitivity which lead them to choose to suppress and deny qualities of the masculine which had formerly guided, directed and ruled timeless and profound cultures before the present? If so, it may take a strong jolt to move them—all of us—out of our "ontological amnesia" (a term used by Mircea Eliade to describe the "loss of being" sometimes suffered by a culture which through defeat or catastrophe loses its center and meaning). Such a jolt may be currently presenting itself in the form of the female patriarch.

Sandra Schneiders, in her book *Women and the Word,* offers a fascinating interpretation of the meaning of Jesus' maleness in our understanding of his message. She maintains and discusses at length that "the maleness of Jesus is theologically, christologically, and sacramentally irrelevant. But the maleness of Jesus is definitely not irrelevant to contemporary spirituality" (p. 56). Schneiders writes that "in a certain sense, Jesus had to be male in order to reveal effectively the true nature of God and of humanity" (p. 58). Her judgment bases itself on the idea that Jesus' message was, in the society in which he lived, associated with the way of life of women and that only in his being a male could the revolutionary power of his gospel be made concrete, visible, revelatory and shocking to those who saw his word exemplified in his life.

Schneiders writes, "Jesus delegitimized the stereotypically male 'virtues' and the typical masculine approach to reality; he validated stereotypically female virtues and lived a distinctly 'feminine' life style" (p. 59). Such a model promoted the mystery of Jesus' teaching and "anchored" it in the experience of those who saw him or heard his message. The power of the resolution of opposites—male and female—which he carried in his person expressed a radical openness to all the members of the family.

Perhaps in our day the rise of women into positions of warriors and builders is a radicalized message of repair, a return to "home" and a way out of our "ontological amnesia." The strange and highly symbolic image of the "female father" may serve as a "whip" to evoke a reconsideration of the patriarchal and the masculine—as indeed it already has in this book.

Women in medicine, in industry, in research and scholarship have demonstrated in increasing numbers the dedication, astuteness, power and knowledge that have over the ages been assigned to the realm of the patriarch. Some women are 'legitimizing' stereotypically masculine virtues and living a distinctly masculine lifestyle. Thus Schneiders's model may be used in its inverse.

The turning of the Wheel has carried the overbalance of yang into the lives of many women where it sometimes may not belong. This is not to say that women cannot effectively or happily express the *patris*. Yet there is undoubtedly a wound in many women partly attributable to forfeiting traditional childbearing and childrearing to carry the yoke of the enfeebled father warrior. Many men have rescinded their lives as *patris* and left the men's house in despair, since the company was drunk, soiled and churlish.

The female patriarch may awaken men to themselves, to the rich realm of the patriarch. Men may discover in themselves the luminous archetypal man slumbering. They may find their way into the father warrior qualities which haunt their dreams and then challenge the current spoiled, cheapened, degraded vision of men, a vision not based on the long rich history of men but on their narrow, insidious portrayal in the recent past.

Part III: Three Male Bodies

The Hunter's Body

We are heirs to three male bodies: the body of the hunter, the body of the builder and the philosopher's body. All three, insofar as they are male, are living the life of the testicles and the phallus, the male brain, the male hands and the male belly. In this the three bodies occupy and function through the same male form, though they are quite different. When they are present simultaneously in the acts and gnosis of an individual, this rare moment may be called *aware kinesis, aware being* or simply *power*.

When I speak of 'body' here I mean soma *and* psyche, the pulsing carnal presence irradiated by image, sensation, reason, clairvoyance, supernal realities and nameless enigma.

If we say "hunter" and "male body," we have essentially spoken in chorus. The chord we have uttered is composed of the cords and sinews which have come into being in resonance with the physical and mythic world (tree, panther, mountain, river) we roamed in and still carry in muscle, bone and tissue: our body is the body of the Pleistocene hunter.

Though this is not the place for a full discussion of this topic, a few words should be said about the foremost patroness of the hunt in Greek mythology: Artemis, a female. I contend that she served as a paradoxical figure much as Jesus (in Schneiders's work cited above) or my "female patriarch" does. That is to say, she inspired men to hunt well, to compete. She herself was vowed to virginity, a vow which many hunters might seek to challenge, though they would fail. Orion, the one male she may have been close to, is said to have accidentally touched her and to have been stung to death by a scorpion for such a pretension. Such dangers greatly inspire awareness and keen senses on the part of the hunter. Also, Artemis's close connection with Zeus as favored daughter created a special contrasexual intercessory (for good or bad) relationship by which the hunter might seek favor with the father—Zeus. She thus serves as a divine anima figure for the hunter—inspiratrix, siren, companion.

The Spanish philosopher Ortega y Gasset writes,

> In order to subsist, early man had to dedicate himself wholly to hunting. Hunting was, then, the first occupation, man's first work and craft. It is exceedingly important to remember this. The venatory occupation was unavoidable and practically the only one, and as the center and root of existence it ruled, oriented and organized human life completely—its acts and its ideas, its technology and sociality. Hunting was, then, the first *form of life* that man adopted, and this means—it should be fundamentally understood—that man's *being consisted first in being a hunter.* If we imagine our species to have disappeared at that point, the word "man" would lack

meaning. Instead of calling that creature "man," we
would have to call him "the hunter." (P. 118)

The hunter's body is male. Males as a group are differen-
tiated physically for the hunt (though some females are built
as hunters). They are tall, heavy, have big bones. They are
constructed for carrying heavy loads: the body of a deer, the
antelope. The Pleistocene male is a fast runner, though none
can catch the jackdaw before he takes flight. Men are developed to be good aimers and weapon throwers. The spear,
the sword, the knife and the club are fitted to be hurled by
the hunter's hand with assurance. Men are deep breathers;
their air sacs are great. Their heavy bones and muscle ar-
mature also hold great protection against physical damage
when the panther turns against them.

Man's existence on the planet has been spent nearly entirely as hunter. The ground of our being is hunting. Quite
recent developments, in the last one percent of human time,
have added new dimensions and new potentials: planting,
the construction of permanent buildings, the dream of
rebirth.

The drive polarity, Eros and Thanatos, arises from the
hunter's animal volition to capture, join and incorporate the
vital other. The unfoldment of art is the meeting of
necessity—that is, the need to discover the animal's mind
so as to capture him, entering him by representing him—
with desire, love and awe of the mysterious form and movements of the creature. Human hands, legs, spine, brain are
those of the hunter poised between the roaming, pulsating
beast and the celestial fathers.

What of modern man eating meat he does not hunt?

A large chest with great capacity which cannot find air to breathe? The lungs cannot be filled. Shallow breathing is nearly a protection against the poisoned air. His lungs, in a chest which once expanded to mirror the expanse of the savannah, the depth of the woods, are now cramped and congested. Running and jogging, once practiced in the pursuit of game or to carry messages back to the tribe, are now practiced in pursuit of that most elusive quarry called "health." Or is it that the hunter has become the game pursued by Death?

The heart, enlarged to pump great volumes of blood to the extremities of the hunter, is now the prey of a stalker called "cholesterol." The word "cholesterol" comes from two words, *chole* and *stereos*. *Chole* (Greek) means "bile" or "gall." *Stereos* means "solid." So cholesterol is a solid bile or solid gall, related to cholera, anger, wrath. Where once the hunter practiced "heart" with his game, depicting it and the hunt on his tipi, on the cave wall, in his songs, now in the heart he is stalked by a solid wrath, by bile. Anger hardens his heart. Wrath stiffens his veins.

An enlarged heart might have increased his capacity for confession, for what James Hillman calls "The Heart of Augustine" (1981), the heart of personal feeling, and also for what he calls "The Heart of Beauty," the heart of imagination. These capacities might have developed in the male more than in the female, and perhaps they have, though they are not expressed as much.

The hardened heart, the heart of coldness, the heart of cholesterol subject the modern man to attack from this organ, and rightly so since, once developed, it will speak in complex speech, as all developed beings do. Its attack will be through the violence of silence. It will not go on beating but will become solid with wrath, hard and cold.

Another possibility for man's salvation, other than running—or perhaps in addition to running, jumping, hunting, using weapons—is that discovered by the Paleolithic man, that is, a movement into the dark, inner caves, to the quieter places, to tell of the hunt, to draw on the walls, to soften the heart, so that the blood may flow. Talk with other hunters; stories told with the Eros of language or art; the discovery of a form of depicting experience, whether through writing in journals or artwork; building a room; repairing an automobile and talking with a friend about it; tending a garden with great care; the enjoyment of literature; the feeling aspects of religious ceremony—all may allow the heart to settle and relax and send its flow deep into the body, its pump renewed, refueled.

Cruelty

The hunter's body—equipped to pursue and capture— always maintains an edge of cruelty, that hewn and polished edge of the tip of the arrow he spends most of his life fashioning.

He edges his spearhead and dreams of bison, imaging in fine detail. He frames each of the bison's powerful movements and muscles in his vision. He envisions and senses the quick and massive shifts of the creature who suddenly chooses between attack and flight. The hunter witnesses the penetration of the worked blade, the severing of sinews, heart, belly and the waning strength of the dangerous animal, his last howls and the heavy fall. The hunter sharpens his weapon to compensate his debility, since he cannot fairly match biceps with the bison's strength. The imagination of the moment of clear strike with the weapon is the birth of *discernment*.

The Hunter's Edge and Consciousness

What separates the hunter from the bison is his edge, his sharpness. He can discriminate among his game, measure and evaluate the bison's speed and strength, and form a critique.

The word "critique" carries within itself the basis of this method. The word is from the Latin root *criticus*, "capable of judging," and from Greek *critos*, "judge," which is cognate with Latin *cernere*, "to sieve, discern, distinguish, understand, and decide." This last grouping of words well describes the various operations which help to unfold a critique: "to sieve, discern, distinguish, understand, and decide." They describe, in an order which is not rigid but generally followed, the development of an act of consciousness.

Sieve

The hunter cuts or breaks a limb of the haw, the maple or elm, choosing for good weight, linearity, taper and tensility. Then he searches for an equipoising flint or quartz to hew and lash as a spearpoint; among the vast rubble, only a few stones will serve, and he sifts among them with care and a fine eye.

Sifting

The discriminating quality, while developed for the bloody reduction of his game, is also aesthetic, as we can see in the vestigial weapons on view (through glass in humidity-controlled atmospheres) in museums.

Sifting is the principle of the hunt, of consciousness and of manhood. The choice of game, of weaponry and of the time of day and season to act are the training and preparation of the hunter, as well as the commencement of individuation. A boy who begins moving to manhood needs above all the operation of sifting, which he learns from his father, the knowledge that he must watch and identify the particulars and their purpose and season among flora, fauna and the living stone. In town or megalopolis this is no less true. The father hunter bears the duty of guiding the son through the fabricated urban wilderness, demonstrating which plants are poisonous, which will sustain, where good hunt may be had, the friendly tribes and the head hunters, the sacred sites, the places of rest and orienting toward home. If the young man cannot sieve the objects and functions of his world, he will not assemble the means or manner of hunting and will stay a boy, become a woman or die.

Discerning

Discerning as an operation means setting qualities apart and perceiving them in their value. The hunter hews his stone blades with a harder rock, one which is more dense and integral but also less able to get and hold a fine edge. One stone for sharpening, one to sharpen, each with its value. The young men who cannot discern the stones will starve; some will learn on their own and will always bear resentment against the father.

The father's job, in part, is the teaching of discernment, telling one thing from another. He recognizes his limits, he presents his best discrimination of good and bad, of right and wrong, of the values which he holds as true. The son may sharpen himself against the father; though he may not choose the same stones to sharpen, he learns a method for choosing.

Understanding

"Understanding" means "standing under." Thus does the hunter come to stand under the Gods, the sky and the animal himself, trembling in his own limits. Father may succeed in the day's hunt. More often he fails, squanders his labors, moves awkwardly, feels fear, misdirects and misaligns himself. This moment, in which the father stands in his bald mortality, *must be witnessed by the son* if they are to have a human relationship. When the son never sees the father at his work, he never sees him in his masculine strength and finitude. *The son must see his father as a failure* before he—the son—can become conscious.

The disappearance of the father into the human community, the community of men, only becomes possible when the son understands his father's failure. Up to the point of failure, the father represents a potential for divinity. He may *be* divine from the point of view of the boy. For a human boy, sonship to a divinity is nothingness. The boy disappears and has no place, no name, no being.

The inevitable failure of the father to represent the divine beings or to represent the community of men in himself is recognized in men's initiation ceremonies. The men of the community, of which the father is only a member— no longer a God—prepare a ritual transformation for the boy. When the father bows to the God to ask forgiveness, to humble himself, he clears a path for the son. Remembering his own arrogance, his own hopes, his own desires for divinity, he recognizes these qualities in his son as natural and ordinary. He knows, with sadness, that his son will one day fail, will one day become human.

He must enter a critique, and the father must stand under this critique as his son stands under him. Failure is the most significant and most specifically masculine human trait, since some failure always accompanies great risk and experiment.

Deciding

The word "decide" arises from Latin *de caedere,* "to cut, hew, lop." This is the most difficult operation because (to use a surgical image) too much or not the right thing may be cut into, severed, removed.

If the hunter over-hunts a species, there will be no more. He cuts boldly and decisively, yet ashamed that he must cut at all. This simple principle guides the father. He rules his son in good measure and with his hands makes decisions the boy will incorporate. Indecisiveness, the attribute of indiscipline, spawns a gelatinous brood.

The hunter demonstrates the power of the weapon, proving to his son that he could murder a herd of elk, and then chooses one animal, praises it, asks forgiveness and kills it, dresses it and returns home with his kill. The son is not to hear of this hunt as an abstraction but tastes the metallic tinge as he licks blood from his fingers, kneeling by the elk. Father's success or failure is unimportant. What the son learns in the field is *decision, cutting* and *humility.*

The primordial structure of pursuit and capture, necessary to all species because they eat and consume, feeding on the life of those beings who coexist on the planet, is borne in the body of the male, in his hands, his lungs, his legs. Civilization has not changed the fundamental ontogeny or the tissue of the body; regardless of the suit which covers the loins of the male body and the colognes which may block the sensing of blood and sweat of the game, the hunter's body will boil for pursuit.

The attempted refusal by the "mind" and endeavor to transform the hunter's body into the gatherer's body confounds the tissue, resulting in lactic burning in the muscles, tension, disease, decay and the deep experience of loss in the male. When the hunter's body is denied extension and release through pursuit and capture of the hunt, the frustrated and denied hands, legs, eyes and lungs will beg the mind for an escalated release from the imprisonment of culture, and *weaponry out of the human hunter's scale* will be required. War-machines and instruments of torture—which are not based on the scale of the hands, the legs, the eyes, the lungs, the testicles—may be viewed as the released aggrandizement and overwrought structures which arise from the frustration of the simple and physically required cruelty of hunting.

When deprived of the hunt of animals—the archetypal need of the body of man—man will hunt man. And for this type of hunt, which is no longer a hunt at all but war (that is, self-hatred projected on other people), the body extends itself to make weaponry which is not to exercise the body of man in pursuit of the escaping animal but to wield death on himself. This is a confusion of magnitude—a brutal misreading of the body's need for participation in the natural cycle of the pursuit and consumption of lower animals.

Suffering

Where it has not been perverted and prevented from expression or driven to cruelty beyond its natural scale, the hunter's body always hesitates and recoils an instant before the infliction of cruelty, and an instant after. All aware hunters feel pain and conscience, observing the still, cooling body of the once vibrant creature.

The word "conscience" means "with" (con) "knowledge" (science); "science" comes from Latin *scindere*, "to cut, to split, divide." What is being split or cleft is the body of the animal he is pursuing. The animal is being cut away from life, and the shared (con) life of the hunter and the animal world is being severed. The hunter momentarily empathically enters the body of the animal and experiences his suffering and death. The conscience he experiences in the presence of the animal is the split in his own bodily presence; the sinews and cords of his own body may be severed as easily as those of the jaguar. The hunter will die and lie inert and emptied as easily as the vibrant gazelle—perhaps more easily. This is the threat Artemis poses. A simple accident may well mean death.

The unfortunate truth is that no one can become a fine hunter without having been hunted or a true father without having been truly fathered. The experience of disillusionment, limits and hot yet sincere argument with him who spawned one is the surest, ablest and best path to conscience, that quality most elusive and most necessary to the *patris*. And no good father wishes upon his son suffering, the death of a lovely vision of peace, the pain of everyday travails, as no good hunter wishes pain on his prey. Yet to deny his son the vital encounter with blood in nature renders the boy feeble, puny, perverse, greedy, immoderate, discourteous and empty of the most virile quality: conscience.

The word "suffering" arises from words meaning "to bear, carry." What the hunter bears is the animal's pain and his own. He asks the animal to fall and die so that he may not, for this moment. The animal therefore collects and bears the cruelty of humankind; bestows, like Jesus, the gift of release from the turpitude of life; and grants the gift of life through his death which is not ours.

The father imposes in like manner the disillusionment, cruelties and wounds of living on the son. One of his responsibilities as a father is to invoke for his son the savagery of the large world through the imposition of limits, controls and confrontations. This is hot instruction, full of tears, boiling and grief, but must be done.

Predation

The hunter is predatory; that is, he seeks to prey on other species, to "plunder" them ("predator" from Latin *pradea,* "plunder"). What is obsessed with escape, he is obsessed to capture; the verb "to prey" is a shortened form of the Latin base *prehendere,* "to grasp, seize, lay hold of." The hunter wishes to touch, hold, to grasp the escaping animal. He wants to eat and consume the fleeing animal, to subsume the qualities of speed, energy, velocity into himself, into his own body. This act carries a tragic aspect because the hunter too is prey—he is well aware—to higher predation which exactly matches the predation his own game suffers at his hands. He will die at the hands of God, the Gods, a stronger enemy, disease, time. What life may be open to him he grasps.

The respectful hunter, therefore, chooses the enchanting animal as the victim of his need and pathos, the requirement of his body to survive and move and have energy.

Where this desire is not proportional—where men have ceased to hunt in human proportion, that is, to hunt lesser animals—it becomes perverse and corrupt. Men invent war and torture—the attempt to take the world of awareness and grasp, seize, lay hold of that which belongs to other human beings; the attempt to take into their hands and destroy their likeness, to destroy themselves. They teach their sons disrespect for human tissue.

The good hunter respects existence and walks with conscience on the living skin of the earth, Mother Gaia; with the shame of his own corruption and miserableness and with awe before the Creator of all tissue, he kills lesser life. The hunter shows his son boldness, joy and proper shame.

Preparation for Death

The hand that lifts and grasps the prey, or touches the still warm belly, and feels the flexible mobility of the tenuous and beautiful coat of the animal carries a signal of wonder to the nervous system of the hunter. It is as if the kundalini serpent were awakened in his chakral body, and he will startle and feel a momentary consciousness unmediated by the various complex rituals in the religious systems of the world.

The hunter enters his own aliveness and mediates with absolute stillness the death of the animal. The ordinary response is to laugh and show his fellow hunters his conquest. He *must* laugh, or the pull to lie down beside the silent and beautiful elk will be too strong. Jorge Luis Borges once remarked that the pull to oblivion is far too sweet, and, therefore, we must rebuke, scorn and hurl abominations on those who speak of it. The hunter cannot forget the moment when his hand touched death, however. Such experience is held alive by *muthos,* story. The hunter must tell of his hunt repeatedly: he must speak of what hands have grasped, the tiredness and cold in his legs and feet, the hunger in his belly, the soreness in his testicles, the long pursuit, the missed shot, the trail of blood, the final moment when a fine long shot was accomplished.

And all hunters must lie; they must invent realities (elements of what we call myth, religion, fiction) because the reality they experience is too awesome and cannot be told. What the hand actually did and how the belly felt at the moment of his eye meeting the eye of the elk is *too present and yet unexperienced.* The hunter does not know and cannot say what he has experienced, because the eloquence of the belly confounds and humiliates speech. Therefore, his speech becomes perplexing, impossible, mysterious. The more this quality is carried—through metaphors which awaken the body and confound the mind—the more we may be aware that the hunter has touched the game with his fearful hand, his hurried breath steamy in the cold air.

Traditional hunting magic holds that animals have masters or overlords under the mountains, deep in the cave or at the bottom of the ocean. Success in the hunt requires permission of these masters to hunt and kill their subjects.

Once, they say, a man did not ask permission of the masters, did not offer up incense and prayer, or ask forgiveness before he hunted. He wounded several animals but did not kill them. Feeling tired late in the day, he fell into a sleep. When he awoke, he found himself surrounded by the wounded animals and their masters. He was told that he must cure all of the wounded animals before he would be allowed to return home and that, thenceforth, he was always to ask permission or his family would not eat again.

This story, this myth—*muthos,* "story"—is the story of Eros binding hunter with the natural world. The story gives a pattern and an understanding of integrity. This hunter was fathered by the animals and their masters to understand his obligation and his relationship to what he kills and what he serves, the world around him.

Fiction, myth, religion, science—these are the ways we tell the stories of who we are. Their languages may be different, but each form of the story creates a mythic view. We can say that the reptilian and limbic systems in the brain are connected with the neocortex, thus binding our earlier evolutionary structures with our later ones. Or, we can say that the hunter fell into sleep and awoke surrounded by the wounded animals. These are both stories told about experience in the tribe, in the family and in the inner man. The stories we tell are passed from fathers to sons and mothers to daughters and, within the various kin of tribe, are our rules, our fathers, the houses and landscapes where we live.

Hunting stories tell us of seasons of weather, the turning and cycling of time, the movement and characteristics and inner life of animals. The hunter learns to become a hunter by a binding empathy revealed in these stories. All tales contain elements of lying and elements of truth. Our measure for judging truth or lie or, better said, our method for judging a story's value in the hunt depends on our allegiance to the stories we love. Stories that we love grant us a key to other stories. They tell us how to read and how to think about and how to experience other stories we hear.

According to Cicero, the word "religion" derives from

relegere, to "go through again in reading or in thought." Ernest Klein believes that this etymology is more probable than one suggested by others who propose a relationship with *religare,* to "link or bind together." Yet both roots of the word tell us something about the effect of religion. In "re-reading" or "re-thinking," we look again on the stories that we love and think about or "read" our experience in their echoes. Our "gospel" is our fiction, our story.

The way we understand our children depends on the way we read seasons, our respect for our animal nature (since children are closer to the masters under the mountain and to instinct than we adults are). The way we pursue our livelihoods depends on our hunting magic, the way we enter the forest, the mountainside. We pursue the game: food, money, achievement. Do we enter asking permission from these sources or masters of our natural world, or do we enter carelessly wounding that which sustains us?

The hunter reads brevity of life and sacredness in his acts. Knowing that life is short and greater than he, he prays for good hunt and for the right to return home. He hunts what he needs and no more and attempts to tell his story well.

A grand story for our culture is painted in that great cave the Bible. In this story, God hunts man incessantly through time, attempting to father him, threatening, propitiating, offering possibilities, but always hunting man to gather him and bring him to his house. That great master under the mountain, Satan, stands at times with the wounded animals around God, who wakes from a trance and is enjoined to cure them. Through the story, man also hunts God, seeking that most elusive of game, the soul. Christ, one of the most conscious of hunters, demonstrates to man and God that each being is hunter and hunted. His rule—do unto others as you would have them do unto you—is the magic granted to cure the wounded animals. His story is the story of hunter and hunted, the inescapable linking of the hunter with the game and the game with the hunter.

Penetration and Penetrativeness

The hunter, like St. Thomas, must place his hand in the wound. This is not so much for belief, which he already has, because he has followed the game, felt the cold, seen the woods, tracks and shadows. Rather, placing the hand in the bloody wound is to support disbelief or mystery. When the hunter's hand is in the wound (this applies to Thomas as well), he participates not more in the "known" but in the "unknown." Two worlds interpenetrate, and the result is not resolution but greater confounding, amazement and surprise.

The body of the hunter experiences sexuality in the same way. (Here I remind the reader that this work is fable, metaphor, a fantasy. I refer to an idealized, evolved, aware hunter. The "historical hunter," according to some writers, was more likely a savage and joyless rapist.)

What he believes he knows—what his body seems to experience as ordinary, present, homeostatic—suddenly becomes shifted. When his lips touch the lips of the beloved woman, he does not understand or believe and an enigmatic cycling of blood and unknown warmth enters his body. Mouth to nipple, the penetration of his penis into the vagina of the woman, the touch of the belly or the thighs of the other transform the hunter's body into an organism of disbelief and mystery. The body of woman, which has escaped him and which at one time he may have believed was game and capture, a kind of prey for him, becomes *in an instant* the huntress, the impossible Artemis, feeding on him, reducing him to a stag but simultaneously rendering to him the body of his transformation, the impossibility of belief and of knowledge and the presence of his own maleness, his phallus, his arms, legs, spine, hot and inescapably present. This moment is represented in Hindu sculpture by Shiva as Lingodbhava—the phallic deity; Rudra, lord of beasts; the creative God of the cosmic dance who emerges from the lingam, the erect phallus.

This is the moment of creation, the sense of being present in the beginnings. The story of the erect phallus is the story of the father's participation in the first things, in serving the masters (Rudra, lord of beasts), recreating the dance of Shiva in sexual dance and frolic.

The Greeks venerated the interpenetrative event through celebrations—most vibrantly demonstrated in Priapus, city named after the God "with the large member"—of the hunter's phallus: in the Phallophoria, a symbolic representation of the pudendum was carried jubilantly through the streets. The humor and goodwill of such a ceremony reveal, as do the lies of the hunter, the sense of wonder and mystery that one experiences in the presence of corporeal reality, as well as the meaning of the meeting and interpenetration of bodies.

Closeness, immediacy, contact and physical experience do not garner more understanding and resolution finally for the hunter. It may seem to him when the flesh is touched that a reduction, an assuagement of his curiosity, has been stated; indeed, some of the body's requirements will momentarily be soothed, but even greater mystery and revelation are transmitted through the awakened hand. The fine eye of the hunter Michelangelo discovers amazement, and the microscope of Watson and Crick, total disbelief, in the form of that finely tuned *muthos,* the scientific theory.

The hunter—the aware hunter—seeks the mystery behind each act. He seeks to discover its season, its movement, its pathways, its "masters." Reverence to the masters behind each act means reverence to the story he loves. This becomes religion: the "re-reading" and "re-thinking" of the story of his hunt is the story of the Great Hunt.

All men entering sexuality, all men entering bodily experience, are hunters of mystery. "The Word became Flesh" is St. John's attempt to formulate the profound contradiction all men experience on discerning that they are corporeal. The last male flight occurs when the adolescent sleeps in the temple of Apollo and dreams that he jumps from the cliffs of Hellespore and soars. All men enter the dream before they fall to stony ground and awaken to bloody, bruised limbs. This bloody reality is sexual, alas, and holds as many soarings and crashings as a male mortal can stand. The father, a raggedy urchin himself, can do little more than pass compassion to his son in the throes of corporeal awakening. His prime gift is humor lovingly admixed of tolerance and self-mordancy, since he himself neither fathoms nor directs soma but lives in its drooling, stenchy throbs. Despite his degrees *Philosophiae Doctor* or *Medicinae Doctor,* the doctor falls trembling without resistance to the first vaguely nubile drab who nears his aura, just as easily as his fourteen-year-old scion, or more easily. He owes his son the honesty of this understanding: his father is victim of flesh, as he is, only more governed by a father's vows.

The Scrotum and the Hunter's Game Bag

The scrotum holds the testicles. The word "testicles" comes from the Latin root *testis,* which means "witness." A facile understanding would render the idea that the testicles witness to "male virility" in the most literal sense of production of sperm, potency for reproduction. In the hunter's body, the testicles witness in the same way that the hunter's game bag does. They witness to, attest to, the fact (from Latin *facere,* "to make, do, act") that the hunter has been in the presence of death and disbelief. The scrotum retracts and recedes into the body during the experience of cold or fear; the hunter recoils before the ferocity of the elements and the infliction of death—yet, he penetrates there because that is the fact (in the sense of "act") of his being.

The bagged game demonstrates that he has been in the country; the word "country" comes from Latin *contra,* "opposite" or "land lying opposite." He has been in the place of opposition, in the land of opposition, where life and death meet. He thus carries his witness, the game bag, wherein lies death. His smile and his stories are laughs from the gallows because he has sought and found death. The testicles, often called "stones" or "balls" or even "eggs" (*huevos,* Spanish), carry the image of the landscape he has traversed (and his father's as well) and also his vulnerability; a male can be easily harmed in the area of his greatest symbolic potency. The testicles are witness to the fact of the hunter's vulnerability and his fertile strength. He moves into the countryside and is wounded, even as he inflicts death or plunders.

Opposition is the father of all awareness. The hunter bears in his body the antinomy of life and death. Plato calls the philosopher a man in love with death; the philosopher is the hunter turned inward. All speculation (*speculae:* "look-ing in"—at the inner being, reflecting) begins with a wound, with dysphoria in the testicles at the discovery of one's animal mortality. Once blood has spilled, nothing can cleanse the stain, and every hunter carries in his game bag proof that our pulse is numbered.

James Hillman writes that

> During the seventeenth and eighteenth centuries reasonable scientific men (Dalepatius, Hartsoeker, Gar-den, Bourget, Leeuwenhoek, Andry), while empirically studying the problems of fertility, conception, and em-bryology, "asserted that they had seen exceedingly minute forms of men, with arms, heads, and legs com-plete, inside the spermatazoa under the microscope." (1972, p. 221)

Such a view, while it does not accord with current ways of perceiving what is within the spermatazoa, tells us more than our current scientific fantasy about what can be seen within the hunter's bag if we look carefully—that is, the preformed entity of life in all its forms living autonomously in the tissue as we ourselves live in the tissue of the biosphere. If we see spermatazoa—and other natural phenomena—simply as an accretion of molecules performing mechanical functions, life becomes an abstraction rather than a relationship. The hunter knows that spermatazoa are indeed sons and daugh-ters, that Odin did create our parents from the trees, that the stones speak and that the Coyote is a brother. His acts on earth are not abstract. What lives in him and in his family lives also in the bear, elk and in the stones in Grand Chaco Canyon.

Scrotum and Belly

In aboriginal tribes the young aspiring warrior is fed the roasted testicles of any enemy killed in battle who demonstrated strength and fortitude even in the face of his own death. The young warrior will absorb into his body the essence of that physical witnessing of death, the condensed testimony carried in those stones; his body will participate in the bodily experience of the dead, and thus honored, warrior. The boy will absorb what he needs to be a father.

What moves to the belly container radiates to the outer limbs. Thus, the hunter attempts to fill his belly with the body of the swift and elusive prey and, thus, becomes hunter and hunted. The testicles produce the fluids with which he hopes to fill his beloved. When he releases his stored essence— through literal body or through the word, called by Aristotle the *logos spermatikoi*—the hunter only apparently penetrates, because he is essentially the captured one. His phallus, once powerfully driven, falls tumescent, and the bag—depleted of live game—hangs drained; the hunter has surrendered his "huevos," the essence of his stones. Regardless of his laughter or his *muthos,* his scrotum (and his belly) becomes emptied. When he resurrects—and life may be defined as a series of resurrections—he may hold to being again and to hunting again; when he no longer resurrects and the belly no longer cries out for its fill, we call this death. What he may hunt there is unknown.

The Hand That Embraces the Weapon

"The hand is the symbol of man's creative power" (Thass-Thienemann, p. 266). When the hand, with all its ability to make, to hold, to soothe and heal (discussed below in "The Body of the Builder"), seizes the weapon, a powerful tension arises. What the hand takes into itself, the club, the knife, the pistol, the rock, it does with naturalness and ease, because the Pleistocene hunter's hand and arm are made for grasping weapons, as the weapons are made for the grasp of the Pleistocene hunter.

An embrace, a handshake, is evoked when the hand grasps the club. Traditional societies carved on the weapon images of the animals to be killed in the hunt: the fish head is carved into the Kwakiutl fish club. Modern weapons are generally more lethal and abstracted. Though a duck gun may still carry the incised stylized image of its prey, the M-16 clearly is an aberration totally unrelated to hunting, bearing only the cold imagery of harm and malice, lacking the vulnerability, imprecision and handwork that is evident in the bow of the Apache, whose primary purpose was hunting (though war was seen as an inevitability and an honor to these men). The hand that grasps the weapon seems not to hesitate, though the belly and the scrotum recoil, remembering as they do the proximity of death.

Fashioning and marking a weapon engage the hand in both pride and shame. A well-made and well-incised weapon is a mark of care, workmanship, awareness and masculine pride. Such a work grants meaning to the act of hunting. Yet a man must traverse the field in shame carrying such weapons. Were his arms, legs and foppish hand stealthy, speedy and powerful as those of the cat, he would need no weapons. Being slow and weak, he recognizes his limits and uses cunning and intelligence to compensate.

Scarcity of Game

Game for the hunter—animals necessarily sought by him as fulfillment of his mythic cycle—has always been scarce. The club and the spear were once inadequate to reduce the abundance of animals available to the hunter; the speed and endurance of the animals put many of them out of man's pitiful reach. As the human arm and hand extended themselves through arrows and then firearms, the animals themselves became more rare. Game preserves—long primarily the *repair* of the rich—began to develop as the hunter became aware of his responsibility to maintain the game, his own body and its need. As urbanization and industrialization have usurped the country, the land and opportunities for hunting have dwindled and become increasingly less accessible.

The Pleistocene hunter now sits in his sad and exhausted body in chromium offices wondering why he is angry, tired and confused. *Exercise, movement, high-speed automobiles, the power of corporate holdings, luxurious surroundings, religious messages, electronic devices, information do not feed the body of the Pleistocene hunter.* They only prove what he already knows—that the game is scarce and that other totally inadequate things are being attempted as substitutes.

The scarcity of game forces the hunter to be alert and aware, to look and see. But the seeing of the hunter is not ordinary seeing. This seeing requires the entire body.

The phrase "the entire body" means also the landscape. The good hunter is not an isolated entity but rather a pulsing organ in the body of field, woods, slope and stream. What comes to pass in the valley and on the outland also moves in the folds and smooths of his own soma. As the pheasant lifts from the maize field, so lift his arms. The trout rises and sips a delicate dun; the hunter's psyche rises. The rabbit who springs from invisibility and bounds is the unbinding of the hunter's moderated pace into jumping and honed alertness.

No game is bagged by the man who reflects on himself in the field as hunter, as king, as pauper, nor by one who has wagered he will stomp and holler in the forest and return home bearing two wild turkeys on his shoulders. *Only the man who disappears can see.*

The hunter is a generalist, skillful, abiding, conserving. He harms no branch through his own choice. Because he peregrinates the body of Mother Earth, the landscape of psyche, he travels awake and sensing and tolerates no malice to nature. Since all is soma, a forest razed is cancer in his tissue. If a sea swamp is drained and a barren and ignominious row of shameless shopping emporiums is erected, he feels the very pool of life drained from his gut and weeps in sorrow for himself and for humankind. Everything in him which is manly, honorable, potent, valorous, just and vibrant recoils in horror at the sight of a chain store with its anile, puerile, fatuous trash for sale.

Urban man has fallen into a murky slumber and sees no more, has vile dreams and poisons himself. Urban man has attempted to forget that he is the Pleistocene hunter and that the particles of his body and his scrotum, hands, belly and eyes carry the unsatisfied and quicksand memory of alert being. All such attempts to refuse attention result in specialization and lethal sciences, looking at single points, an activity which rots the eyes and inflames the prostate and leaves the belly large and puffy but empty. What passes before his

eyes—nearly everything but the single object of his vision—
will be missed. No game is to be sighted, and yet his blood
boils and shoots his eyes full of their weakened substance.

He no longer believes he is a hunter; he no longer believes he is male; he no longer yearns for woman or the interpenetration of the hunt. He no longer believes in the
country, the land of opposites, and—far from answering the
call of the scarcity of game—he collapses into his bed early
or always, believing the hunt is finished. His body awakens
and travails to resurrect while he sleeps, confecting images,
dreams full of scrotums and phalluses, bellies, eyes, arms,
hands, weapons and jaguars. He awakens sweating and damns
his dreams and believes he should consult the doctor. He
falls asleep again and dreams that the doctor is a panther.
When he startles awake a second time, he stumbles to the
medicine cabinet and swallows heavy sedatives. The reviled
pump—his heart—finally settles and freezes. Having hunted
himself, he lies down inert, unperceived by the hunter himself, evanescent, ephemeral, null.

Yet if he finds his world reduced, he may still track life
in this landscape. Cynicism, while always present and honed
as an edge of discernment, accompanies a wider vision as
well. Awakening among the wounded animals with the charge
of curing them and himself, he seeks a new understanding
of the modern hunt.

One landscape in which he hunts is in the interior of
his own being. Tracking there he will find visions, nightmares,
his inadequacies, his fears, his sorrows, his griefs. These
animals are tracked in memory. The bones of experience
are gathered and given life again. He tracks his history by
remembering, by holding images shimmering and alive. He
looks at his boyhood, his sonship, his father's sternness. He

remembers punishment, moving from one house to another, losing a best friend; recalling his sadness, he becomes the boy again, small and wounded. He stands before himself, asking to live. He recalls the severing pain of being torn from the dark womb, the dark warm cave, and discovering that he is not she and must act on his own; his baby is brought to life before him terrified, requiring the hunter's fatherly arms. His many failures and successes, the boys and men he has been stand calling for his attention. Attending to them, hearing the grief, the complaints, terrors, excitements of each, he asks their forgiveness and that of their master. He re-stores—re-stories—himself by gaining his history, the stories of his hunt. Then he begins to tell his story to other hunters. This is what I saw; this is what I experienced. These are the animals I have wounded, come to demand cure.

The next wounded animals that appear to him are those of his family. The betrayal from his brother, the loss of his father, the times he hit his son in fury, the many cycles of gaining and losing his wife, the hatreds, rages and violations committed by him as by any human being—all come out to stand around him, demanding cure. Attention—that is to say, religion, the re-reading and re-thinking of his story and the story of the family—regains a lost landscape. His family and he are told the same story. A uniting and relief come for all members of the hunt.

In the world of the markets, his vision, his extraordinary seeing, encounters a great challenge, since the wounded animals are so many. Where the forest was and now the shopping mall stands, he still must find the forest. He must eat; he must have clothing; he must house and shelter his family. Asking permission and forgiveness, he enters the shopping mall, seeking a product.

"Product," from *producere*, "to lead or bring forth," is something begotten, brought forth, made, created. Most of the products he finds, if not all, are begotten wounded, ill-conceived, manufactured—that is, "made by hands"—which are impersonal and careless and tell the story of the search for high profits, efficiency and high quantity. Occasionally, he finds a product begotten with care, attention and respect. This product he rescues, takes home and treats with the honor due a well-conceived thought made concrete.

The poorly attended product, its seams not fitting, its material inert, its function or usage brief, halting, suspect— this may be all that is available to him. These products require greater attention, greater care, greater patience, since they are more wounded. Objects made of plastic or other synthetics have great difficulty returning to the earth, to their masters; therefore, their wounds are greater, as they have been transformed by hunters with little or no respect for their natural landscapes. These products require great imagination in order to remain animate, useful, alive.

Businessmen, politicians, teachers, health care workers, retail shop owners, engineers, carpenters, mechanics, soldiers, artists, clergymen—all of us have bulldozed the forest, sealed the caves, disregarded the ancient rite of asking permission before the hunt, tried to ignore the wounded animals, laughed at masters. Some men may begin to awaken from the trance. Already the wounded animals are gathered in the streets, in the hospitals, in the supermarkets. Doesn't every aluminum can in its cast metal contain the scream of a tree torn from the ground in a rain forest?

The Body of the Builder

The builder's body inhabits and is inhabited by a country (a land of oppositions), as is the hunter's body. The longing for participation in the tissue experience of the animal—hunting, escape, capture, death, consumption—is accompanied in the body by another deep longing: to participate in the still, eternal life of the plant, whose movement is slow, internal, absolute, inevitable. The two primary acts of the builder's body are separation and unification. Separation means the acts of destruction of the vegetative world by which the builder demonstrates his distance from that world. Unification means the acts of joining and making by which the builder attempts to re-enter his antediluvian origin.

Separation is an act of severing, rending apart, discerning, and, like the weapon fabrication of the hunter, it requires a critique. In separation, the life of the limbs is lived. Separation requires climbing, cleaving, pulling, pushing, sawing, hacking, grinding, lifting, hurling and hauling away. It is entirely a matter of assertion and lumberjackery. Separation may be practiced in an addlepated, thrashing, brutish, cowardly, unconscious manner through blind hacking; or separation may be practiced in a manly, fatherly way, with potency, solicitude, humility, diligence and shepherding, as well as from the view that, despite his most honest effort, the builder performs his lacerations in plain ignorance. Wherever he cuts a forest or tears away a boulder, he has inevitably done harm.

Unification is the builder's chance at penitence. Where his construction kneels before the subtle dowry of the vegetative world, he gains integrity, substance and a nexus to the pith and roots of the raw, divine world. This is the only salvation accessible in our breathing days, and the builder is the seeker of heaven, the abode of bliss. He wishes to build paradise.

Gary Snyder has developed in his poetry, in his commitment to land and in his religious perspective this sense of separation and unification. The title poem of his book *Axe Handles* suggests some images and patterns from the body of the builder:

> One afternoon the last week in April
> Showing Kai how to throw a hatchet
> One-half turn and it sticks in a stump.
> He recalls the hatchet-head
> Without a handle, in the shop
> And go gets it, and wants it for his own.
> A broken-off axe handle behind the door
> Is long enough for a hatchet.
> We cut it to length and take it
> With the hatchet head
> And working hatchet, to the wood block.
> There I begin to shape the old handle
> With the hatchet, and the phrase
> First learned from Ezra Pound
> Rings in my ears!

"When making an axe handle
            the pattern is not far off."
And I say this to Kai
"Look: We'll shape the handle
by checking the handle
Of the axe we cut with—"
And he sees. And I hear it again:
It's in Lu Ji's *Wen Fu,* fourth century
A.D. "Essay on Literature"—in the
Preface: "In making the handle
Of an axe
By cutting wood with an axe
The model is indeed near at hand."
My teacher Shih-hsiang Chen
Translated that and taught it years ago
And I see: Pound was an axe
Chen was an axe, I am an axe
And my son a handle, soon
To be shaping again, model
And tool, craft of culture.
How we go on.

                              (Pp. 5–6)

The handle of the axe is what we seek to grasp. The pattern of grasping in this poem is the pattern of fatherhood. The desire of the son who wants an axe of his own evokes the desire of the father to shape, to create, to make a place for his son. Snyder's fathers, such as Ezra Pound, his teacher Shih-hsiang Chen and language, give him their patriarchy. The shaping of the axe handle is the unifying and bodily principle in this joinery between father and son.

The very tool of separation, the axe, is separated in the

son between an axe handle and a hatchet head, the body and the mind, if we think reductively. Or that which we grasp and that which severs. What were disparate parts, cut from this place and that, are now joined. The hatchet head is joined with an axe handle, now cut to its proper dimensions. We may think back here to the image of "pattern," of "father as rule." What is measured and brought into proportion is a handle, that which we grasp, that which we hold.

Also joined are literature and language with wood, metal and purpose. Shaping thought, shaping story, shaping our reading of experience, shaping relationship between patriarchs and between the personal father and the young warrior, the act of building connects. What was wounded, torn or cleft now may be joined, brought into a pattern and stood under.

Standing with Snyder is the God Hephaistos, the cripple cast down by his mother, laughed at by the Gods, wounded, yet the great builder, forger, craftsman. What we forge in the world is story. Hephaistos has built the great palaces for the Gods. Out of his suffering he becomes the artisan. What we use to fabricate in the world—the tools, materials, the qualities of our own bodies—becomes the elements of our building, our patriarchy.

C. G. Jung offers models to the builder, discovering in his landscape the disparate tools of medicine, psychology, literature, anthropology, alchemy. He held them in his life, not as a unified, finished system or structure, but as an animate growing body of contradictions, suggestions, metaphors, broadly hewn bricks and boards held together through the dynamism of fascination.

Jung's work is often known through its translators, through the "summarizers," not in its original form. His own vision (which he himself betrayed at times) was not to build a system, but rather an "attitude toward the psyche," toward psychological experience.

The most concrete image of Jung as "Father Builder" is in his retreat, his Tower at Bollingen. The Tower was built gradually over the period of thirty-four years and became a "second body," a masculine womb, for Jung. He writes:

> At Bollingen I am in the midst of my true life, I am most deeply myself. . . .
>
> At times I feel as if I am spread out over the landscape and inside things, and am myself living in every tree, in the plashing of the waves, in the clouds and the animals that come and go, in the procession of the seasons. There is nothing in the Tower that has not grown into its own form over the decades, nothing with which I am not linked. Here everything has its history, and mine; here is space for the spaceless kingdom of the world's and the psyche's hinterland.
>
> I have done without electricity, and tend the fireplace and stove myself. Evenings, I light the old lamps. There is no running water, and I pump the water from the well. I chop the wood and cook the food. (1961, p. 225)

The builder chooses the place, and the place chooses the builder. There is an interpenetration between the two which is sacred. The builder reads in the landscape, in the materials, in the design and the construction a form of story and a form of thought. The house he builds, the stories he assembles and uses as his own, his religious practices and the form of relationship he chooses to make with other people are all aspects of the way he builds for the inner man, for the outer man, for his family and for the culture. When his edifices are towers of trash, the builder enters hell, where the pay is good.

The Concreteness of the Vegetative Body

Thass-Thienemann writes,

> . . . the body self, being the most concrete reality, came to be the realization of the concept of concrete which properly means "grown together," from the L. *con,* "together," and the participle of the verb *creco, ere, cretum,* "to grow." One may ask, what has grown together? In the unconscious fantasies each member was first an independent entity, which afterward grew into one body. There still remained a strife and competition between the former independent members. The word part, from the L. *pars, partis,* means "part of the body," especially, the genitals. The word part is a derivative of the Latin verb *pario, ere, partum,* "to give birth." (P. 264)

The body so perceived is as a garden, a vegetative grouping of elementorums which grow together, join darkly in the deep roots, vine together in the sun, become fused in the midst of competition and striving for sunlight, perdurance and territory. A slow, milling oppositionalism prevails in the vegetative world and in the builder's body. However much the green density draws to fusion, the builder's body wrestles for consciousness and a place outside of the tangled tubers. One activity which demonstrates this is the primordial act of naming.

The Builder's Body and the Tree

The male body and the tree have a rich brotherhood in the collective treasurehouse. Men are said to have come down from their aboriginal home in the trees. Man and tree look alike. Thass-Thienemann again:

> . . . the male organ became denoted in almost all our languages by a reference to a "twig" cut from the tree. On the conscious level, the "rod, twig, piece of wood" is named but it is by the unconscious fantasies that the male organ is understood. Such examples are the Greek *hrapis,* "rod" is Latin equivalent *verpa,* meaning "membrum virile" (feminine!), *verpus,* "circumcised man." The Latin *virga* means "twig" and "penis" (feminine!), the derivative French *verge* also covers both meanings. So does the German *rute,* "rod" (feminine!). The English *rod* also has this double reference to man and tree; in the United States slang it also denotes "pistol." (Ibid., p. 101)

The seemingly strange fact that many of the words which relate to the male organ are feminine may be understood as a recognition of the confusion in the male hunter who finds himself suddenly tangled in a world of vegetative growth often more closely associated with the female body. Alternately, the penis may be understood as that part of the man which enters the dark feminine and contributes thus to the *pario,* giving birth to the body in its concreteness.

The tree, then, in its uprightness, its strength and separation from the dark entanglement, presents itself as a herm — that image of the phallus used in part to point directions on roads in Greece in the mythic era (Leach)—to the builder. The tree, as substance, direction and model for the maker, offers its body as possibility and form to resonate in the body of the builder.

Men have also been known to live in the trees, as they live in their own bodies, thus creating a dual illusion, a confoundment and a rich source of metaphor and *muthos*. Fowles writes:

> One of the oldest and most diffused bodies of myth and folklore has accreted round the idea of the man in the trees. In all his manifestations, as dryad, as stag-headed Herne, as outlaw, he possesses the characteristic of elusiveness, a power of "melting" into the trees, and I am certain the attraction of the myth is so profound and universal because it is constantly "played" inside every individual consciousness.

I would add that it is "played" in every man's body as well, for the male hides in his body and yet presents himself inevitably in his maleness and as tree-body, though many men currently may attempt to present themselves as other types of foliage.

As for Fowles's word "played," it is interesting to note with Thass-Thienemann that it contains an explicit male sexual reference. He writes, "The English *play* is . . . explicit. It means, besides 'to move freely within limits,' primarily 'to move swiftly, erratically, to and fro'; it also means 'to discharge, eject or fire something' " (p. 280). The quality of union between (joining) of animal and vegetable world is thus embodied in the image of tree and phallus by the reference to "play"; though the vegetative tree provides the durability and erectness, the animal phallus provides the swift movement.

Gautama Buddha was incarnated forty-three times as a tree and attained bliss under the Bo Tree. We may take solace in the number of times Buddha had to enter the core body before he would awaken under its tabernacle.

Our primordial parents were trees transformed by Odin. The date palm and the pine cone are venereal. Hesiod held that men were born of ash seeds. Our progenitors are immortal, being trees. The house is a transfigured tree. According to the Koran, the Tooba Tree stands in Paradise replete of fruit, springs flowing water, milk, honey and wine. The Jinn of Arabia were said to inhabit the trees. Trees have given both home and sanctuary to the wayward and the recondite. The builder, working with wood, works with his body, his mythic history and his family.

The architect Christopher Alexander describes in his work an attitude of respect for the interpenetration of body, family, nature and history, which he calls "the timeless way of building." Seeking a description of the fundamental quality or qualities of this way of building, Alexander posits numerous terms, such as whole, comfortable, free, balanced, eternal. Each of the terms, he decides, is insufficient when taken singly.

Certain qualities have to do with a relationship forged between the builder and the place. In speaking of the quality of wholeness, he describes trees along a wild and windblown lake:

> These trees and branches are so made that when the wind blows, they all bend. All the forces in the system, even the violent forces of the wind, are still in balance

when the trees are bent. And because they are in balance, they do no harm, they do no violence. The configuration of the bending trees makes them self-maintaining. (1979, p. 35)

In another passage, Alexander characterizes the process of building placement as one of precision, yet made up of many variables. He depicts the act of making a table in his garden for feeding blackbirds in the winter. He wants a table at which they will feed freely. He writes,

But it is not so easy to build a table that will really work. The birds follow their own laws and if I don't understand them, they just won't come. If I put the table too low, the birds won't fly down to it because they don't like to swoop too close to the ground. If it is too high in the air or too exposed, the wind won't let them settle on it. If it is near a laundry line blowing in the wind, they will be frightened by the moving line. Most of the places where I put the table will not work.

I slowly learn that blackbirds have a million subtle forces guiding them in their behavior. If I don't understand these forces there is simply nothing I can do to make the table come to life. So long as the placing of the table is inexact, my image of the blackbirds flocked around the table eating is just wishful thinking. To make the table live, I must take these forces seriously, and place the table in a position that is perfectly exact. (Ibid., p. 36)

Later, considering the word "exact," he substitutes "egoless," a word meant to guard the aliveness and the interrelationship between the builder and the place. He writes that "the quality that has no name includes these simpler, sweeter qualities, but it is so ordinary as well that it somehow reminds us of the passing of our life. . . . it is a slightly bitter quality" (ibid., p. 39).

The body a man is building when he lives, works and plays is psyche, soul. This is not a spooky, spirit, transparent entity but an entity of that which passes and that which remains. The epicenter of the body, that is the place of greatest impact, is everywhere. Every action implies separation and unification. What we do in work builds the soul. What is meant by right livelihood is the use of our tools—our mind, our physical form, our emotions—to build the place where the story we love occurs.

When we build a house, a relationship, a family, we build according to the instructions in the story we love—or against it, out of greed or hate. It may seem odd that a builder might construct according to a story he hates or disrespects, yet many build according to such specifications.

The finest materials for building a family are trust, respect and loyalty. When well forged, these materials are eternal. They live long past the builder. Of course, all construction outlives and predates a single life. It is the duty and obligation of the patriarch of each generation to assure the use of the best available materials and to build according to his best skill. We may paraphrase Jesus: build for others as you would have them build for you.

The body constructed in work is a body inseparable from the body of play. Doing, making, creating, regardless of the form each takes, carry their own intrinsic material. Hillman writes: "The hands themselves *want* to do things, and the mind loves to apply itself" (1983, p. 167).

Work is a matter of building with hands and mind. What we build with hands and mind, the story of work, is the story of community, the community building. What we build when we work is an axis running through from the inner man, the physical form, the family, the tribe and the culture. When the construction of buildings was slower and more tedious, it was easier to see the contribution of each generation to the building of great cathedrals. In the life of an individual, the construction of a cathedral had a feeling of eternity, since it was rarely finished during the span of that life. The sense of the continuity of working, of builder building on grandfather's work, was visible, graphically present at all times.

The Builder's Sacrificial Body

Though the builder experiences in the tree his own body, he must cut and clear it to make space and to yield material for construction. The primary building materials for man have been trees and stones. Thus, he must perform a castration on the body from which he has taken form. His first act is to grasp the axe, the hoe, the saw and the pick and to create separation, to discriminate among parts and tear them away from the vegetative body. The discrimination of parts is a very subtle operation and, I believe, is (because improperly practiced now) the source of the great, ponderous ugliness in the bodies of our modern cities and (because formerly practiced with reverence) of the timeless beauty and deep patriarchy of the pueblo, the traditional village, the ancient river settlement. The broad and rending swath of the large machine allows little discrimination. *When tools can no longer be lifted and carried by the human hand and their weight felt and manipulated by the builder's muscles, he forgets that he is destroying his body, castrating himself.* It seems ironic that the steel and glass structures of the modern city, whose materials seem to participate so fully in the separation of the builder from the vegetative world, have actually fallen into a chaos, an undistinguished and tangled amorphism which bears no connection with the builder's body, shows no mark of his hand, does not breathe, has no belly, no scrotum, no phallus.

The traditional structure—such as the log cabin, the teepee, the pueblo, European cathedrals built over centuries—always speaks: *the hand touched here; touch this belly and you will feel it.* The glass and steel edifices, for example, the Sears Tower in Chicago, though awesome and monumental, cannot be touched. Such offices cannot be penetrated; no myth can accrete around men who live there because *no man lives in his being there, nor could he, nor would he want to.* The true builder builds his own body, and the structure he makes results from cleaving and suffering and his sweat and will always remind those who draw near of the vegetative body, the tree, the hand, the belly and the scrotum of the builder. Jesus was bound to the tree, demonstrating the sacrifice of the male body and its tie with the tree.

The Unified Body

Having discriminated and cut away the parts of the vegetative body he is going to use, the builder attempts to reconstruct his body whole. He wants to become the family, to construct the family and house, the *dh-mo,* to enter his own origins, to become his own antediluvian father. His hand extends itself in the form of tools, a word which arises from the root *tawain,* which means "to prepare."

Adze and saw, shovel, hoe and hatchet all stand inert

as part of the pre-paration (pre-birth). The house, the shed, the gate, the teepee—all remain quiescent as *eidolan* in the archetypal conception of the builder. Only the hand, the eyes, the belly, the legs, the scrotum, the ligaments and muscles, the pump coursing throughout the builder can serve to bring the *eidolan* to embodiment. The embodiment, the enacted and physical presence wrought and touched by the body of the builder, is a high and great mystery, since embodiment is the work of the Gods, while mere mortals may only dream.

The hand grasps the plane firmly while the shoulder, the chest, belly and legs lean with a measured weight to smoothe and level. The eye watches carefully and then mandates the hand to run along the side for validation of the edge just planed. The binding of rope to make ligaments, the enclosing of space to form the belly, fireplace and chimney for the transfigured stones and phallus, pitch poured or pelts stretched to make the skin—the builder's body (his *dh-mo*) takes form. As the builder makes the bishop's crosier, so he creates the minaret, the tower, the bridge and even the casket, which is a final layer of skin added in an attempt to extend the life of the body.

Whatever the builder makes, he creates from his own body, from the world encompassed within his *vital circle.* Ortega y Gasset reminds us that "yo soy yo y mis circunstancias": I am I plus my circumstances, what *The Secret of the Golden Flower* refers to as the "midst of conditions." What my body encompasses, "yo y mis circunstancias," is the *country* from which I take my material and from which I may create my house, my family, the unified body.

Containers, Vessels, Belly, Scrotum

We have already spoken of the testicles as witness in the hunter's body to the presence of cruelty, suffering, pursuit, capture, death and consumption. In the builder's body, they are witness to separation and unification, the accretion of materials into form, storage and containment. One image which carries the *kinesis* of the builder's body into form is that of the potter fashioning his vessel, the body lifted from the chaos of the lump of clay into the enlivened cavity which creates a tension of spaces: inner and outer. Philip Rawson writes:

> . . . container pots are normally felt to consist of a number of fundamental parts. The way that these parts are related to each other, the proportions they are given, their scale in relation to the human being and his hands, and the relation of one part to the others constitute a major element in ceramic expression. And it is no accident that we, as well as other peoples, have always used anthropomorphic terms to designate these different parts of the pot, which is seen to be, in some sense, a symbolic analogue of the human body. There is, thus, a powerful element of somatic suggestion in the proportions and relations between the parts of pots, which can only be felt, not really described. Only rarely do pots have heads. . . . But they all have "lips." And this term (labia in Latin), defining two orifices symbolically connected with those of pots, is most significant in view of the general female quality . . . for container wares. (1984, p. 100)

The main parts of the pot are usually described thus: 'belly'

for the main bulk container; 'foot' for the supporting element, either a mere ring or a high pedestal, 'stem' if it is
long and narrow; 'shoulder' for the point at which a shape
turns over at the closure; 'neck' for a developed form giving
on to the interior; 'lip' for the shape which encircles the rim.

The vessel is a specialized and clear instance of the purpose to which the builder's body is put in all cases—that
is, the fashioning, from the separated *parts* of the world which
lie in a seeming chaos, of a body which extends in space and
which reflects his own body.

Assemblage and Body Parts, Male Healing, Repair

What is disparate, dismembered or fallen apart may be
joined. This is the outmost generalization and mystery of
the builder's body, the invocation of the constructor, the doctor, the artist and the teacher. The prime mystery is the extension of the body of the *patris* to draw chaos into pattern.

According to Hesiod, Chaos is the original Goddess
from whom Erebus, Nyx (Night), Tartarus and Eros are born.
One of the first divine beings to emanate from Chaos, Eros
is the source, the Father, of connections, ties, harmonies and
congress between people and between people and the
natural world. Without Eros, men are monads without relation. Without Eros, objects lie like galactic islands, lifeless,
cold, mechanical. Eros joins, like the carpenter, builds the
structure of the love affair and the family, builds the house
from whatever materials are available both from the psyche
and from the field. If mud and straw, an adobe; if ice, an
igloo; if cardboard, a shanty; if long pine, a lodge. Some men
live in streets and build a house of the flow of traffic, blood

and gism; some make a family with Mary, sackcloth and an altar; there are men who live wholly on rivers, in caves, in condominiums, in row houses in Indianapolis; there are men who build houses of desire or of nightmares. Eros draws out of Chaos into pattern whatever lies about; all men muster an existence, an assemblage of the miscellany of their moments.

Erebus (Darkness) is the father of Hemera (Day) and Aether (Air) by Nyx (Night). So Darkness fathers Day and Air, bringing visibility and breath into the world; what is diffused, disparate, unbounded and indistinct is brought into clarity, lightness and connection. The builder, through skill and endurance, makes a structure.

Male birth and male healing are thus performed by the builder through his use of the materials and contingencies— the "circunstancias"—he encounters. Regardless of the objects, the parts given to him, though, and the elements of which they are made, the builder will need to return to his body—his belly, phallus, hands, eyes, scrotum—to find witness for the patterns which will relate "yo y mis circunstancias." His archetype, his guide and *pater,* is the tree and, to a lesser extent, the stone. These are his templates. So long as he uses the pattern of body, tree, field, mountain and river and treats the eye, the flesh and the fingers with the delight of what is given in the innate tide of the vibrant earth, he will live in his *dh-mo,* his being, house, family.

When he has lost his proper reverence and reference to these—as the builder frequently seems to have in our day—he has lost his male body, his relation with woman, his family, his rule and his being.

The Builder's Place

The builder's voice has a sense of place, its own time, a sense of wonder and of the touch of materials. The builder speaks of his body, of what rules him and what he needs to live and endure. Wendell Berry writes in his poem "The Sycamore,"

In the place that is my own place, whose earth
I am shaped in and must bear, there is an old tree growing,
a great sycamore that is a wondrous healer of itself.

(P. 65)

The builder, like Berry's sycamore, heals by placing himself and enduring.

How does builder select place, or it him? Where is modern man to build the foundation of the future generations? What place does a father make for his sons and daughters?

The old ones, the grandfathers of various traditions, teach how to find a place and how to be selected by a place, how to build, what to build and with what materials. Foundation rites, practiced widely throughout Europe, Africa and Asia, offer their story to us, a blueprint for the builder in a particular place.

The first moment in the rites is choosing the site. The grandfather builder approaches a place with three main considerations. First, what it offers to his occupation: is there clay nearby; are there good woods nearby; is the land good for farming, for hunting? What are the trade routes; are there markets for the goods? Second, what are the animal omens? What animals have passed the place? Do they pass in groups or singly? Do they appear as they appeared in the dreams of last night? How are they related to the animal guardians, the animal spirits? Enemies or friends? Third, what is the story of the place? Is the story good? Has this place had a story of success? a good past? Are the mythical beings and ghosts that wander this territory friendly or hurtful? In the story, how have people been harmed? Have they enjoyed a happy relationship with the other world, with the Gods, with the grandfathers of the place?

A restlessness haunts modern man, especially the American man, an urge to move, never to choose or be chosen by a place, never to root into its ground. This is for good reason. We have lost the methods of knowing and attending to the mythical beings of a location. The stories we tell and are told about a place are primarily lies. Think of locales: Santa Fe, Northern California, Oregon, the heart of Montana, the Adirondacks. These are a few among many, many places with an enormous healing power and a story of healing. Yet healing cannot take place if the story is not the story of the builder. One cannot become an Anasazi by visiting the Mesas or a Kwakiutl by living in the verdant forests of the Olympic Peninsula. Are we doomed to be a nation of nomads? Perhaps. America has yet to be settled by the Europeans, Orientals, Africans and other "foreigners" who live here.

An important step in the choice of a place to build is to stop moving. The spot where the builder stands is the center of the world, the place of emergence and the center of the labyrinth. When the Hopis built the kiva, the men's house where ceremonies and lounging and conversation took place, it was made to be entered through the top by a ladder. Climbing down into the kiva, one would find a spot in the base of the room, a carved niche, a hole into the earth.

This is the *shipapu,* the place of emergence, where men came up from below the earth to make life on the surface of the world. This is the place of the beginning of our world. Each place the builder stands, it is possible to make the *shipapu,* the place of emergence. A small altar is built in the *shipapu* and then closed over, a recognition of the beginnings.

All places have their story and their spirits emerging. Each place is a story of weather, of beauty and ugliness, of the effects of the ages past, of success and failure, of war, of the communities, of dangers, of security. To discover the story of the place where the builder stands is to discover himself within the story of the place.

Every place has its story of emergence—how the place and its particular inhabitants came into this world; each place has its genesis just as the world has its genesis. Settlers came and found a world, and it was or was not what they were seeking. The original inhabitants and their Garden: each place has its pristine age, its golden time before our time. The miners arrived to dig into the mountain, the hunters arrived killing the buffalo, a massacre occurred here once, Coyote walked here, Jesus walked here, Paul Bunyan rode Blue here; Willard Johnson plowed here for eighty years; once the humans came up from underground, or from beyond the sea or from Atlantis, and emerged here and brought these things and this knowledge. Mrs. Quigley of Eureka Springs, Arkansas, burned down the house when her husband refused to build it as she had designed. One day she moved the kids and all the major possessions out of the house and just burned it down. When he returned from the field, he found it smoldering and had to rebuild—the house of her design.

The second image of place develops, that is, the labyrinth, once the time of emergence has taken place. One often-told story of the labyrinth involves Minos, son of Zeus and Europa. King of Crete, he was the husband of Pasiphae, who was daughter of the Sun, Helios. A bull came up from the ocean to be sacrificed by Minos. He did not sacrifice it, and his wife became inflamed with an insatiable passion for the bull. She asked Daedalus, the master craftsman, to build her a wooden cow into which she entered, offering herself to the bull to satiate her lust.

Enraged by this act and also because of the murder of his son Androgeos at Athens, Minos commanded this same Daedalus to construct a labyrinth. The child of the abnormal passion between Pasiphae and the bull, the Minotaur, half man, half bull, was placed at the center of the labyrinth. Minos forced the Athenians to send an annual tribute of seven virgins and seven youths to be driven into the labyrinth and devoured by the Minotaur.

Theseus of Athens, a young warrior, volunteered to enter the labyrinth to kill the Minotaur. With the help of Ariadne, Minos's daughter, he murdered the monster and escaped, taking Ariadne with him, only to abandon her on Naxos, inflamed with a passion for Phaedra, her younger sister. On returning to Athens, he was to change his black sail for a white one to signal to his father that he was alive and victorious. He forgot, however, to change the sail. His father, seeing a black sail, threw himself off a cliff and died.

Daedalus, meanwhile, was forced with his son Icarus to the center of the labyrinth, from which there was no escape. Fashioning wings from wax and the feathers of birds, he and his son flew out, Daedalus landing safely and Icarus flying too near the sun. The wax in his wings melting, he fell in the sea and drowned.

Just as all places have their quality of center of the world, the place of emergence and place of creation, they all as well embody the labyrinth. The labyrinth, in this Greek story, the built labyrinth, is but the visible manifestation of the labyrinth inside each person and the one built with such intricacy *among* persons.

Minos has the labyrinth built to sequester and entrap the product of his wife's passion. The loss of his son he attempts to revenge through the sacrifice of the young and innocent of Athens. To craft this attempted entrapment of time, he engages Daedalus, whose name means "to build well." The son of Hephaistos, he is a master maker. All builders attempt, if they have integrity, to freeze time, to capture its essence within the labyrinth of the built structure. Minos may have learned, had he been able, from the Hopis, who place at the center the *shipapu*, the place of emergence, that mythic beings and new life may return at any moment from where we stand.

With the help of the daughter of Minos, Theseus enters the labyrinth to kill the Minotaur; he can find his way into the labyrinth, he can kill the Minotaur, and, with help, he can get out. But the labyrinth extends far beyond the visible one. When he is attracted to her sister, he ungratefully forgets his commitment to Ariadne, who had helped him accomplish his task of slaying the Minotaur. His forgetfulness, that is, his not remembering to change the sails, is what prompts the suicide of his father, who jumps to his death in grief. Thus his father, his own sense of fatherhood—his sense of being rule and order—is lost and dies through self-destruction.

His fault is the opposite of Minos's. Minos forgets the place of new creation, the place of emergence. Theseus does not know that the labyrinth is everywhere and re-enters it through temptation and forgetfulness. He becomes an abductor of women; he carries Helen off from Sparta as a girl; he aids Pirithous in his attempt to abduct Persephone from Hades; he is trapped in the labyrinth of a pattern, that of abduction, of usurping. He never settles into his own place.

Daedalus, like all builders, built the labyrinth within which he himself would be imprisoned, with his son. He had made the object of desire which drew the bull to Pasiphae to pacify her lust, the wooden cow which was the construction of a labyrinth of desire. When this was used, it provoked the wrath of Minos—wrath toward his wife and toward youth. Daedalus built a place of desire and also a place of sacrifice and death.

When the builder selects a place to build, he must know that it will be at the center of the world and also a labyrinth; that his reasons, plans and purposes will meet those of other people and their story, the stories of ghosts, spirits and mythical beings that inhabit the place. These are inescapable. Each site is mythic and deserves honor and respect. A place heals and is healed to the extent it is honored by its inhabitants.

The healing of a place and being healed by a place have to do with the extent to which Eros, that God of binding and connecting, is present. America, and especially the American West, was once a virgin land which had its own extraordinary beauty. For modern Americans, for most of us, whether we live in one of the great cities, in towns or countrysides, that beauty has disintegrated into disorder, chaos, stories of brokenness, of rubble, of too quickly built buildings, of cities and towns coming apart. These broken, rubbished, salvage-yarded places are the centers of labyrinths. The locus of emergence, the *shipapu*, is somewhere in the brickpile; can we clear it away so that the new builder spirits may emerge?

Relations gone sour, families in crisis, divorces, fundamental mistrusts, betrayals, battles between men and women, the misgivings of a woman attempting to control a company in a male-dominated industry—these are places of labyrinth. The place of emergence is down at their base. Isn't a family in crisis one which is looking for a new spirit and forgetting its old stories? Then tell the old story, bring it out—not so the family can "communicate," which sounds like a punishment, but so that the story can be told.

Down in the belly of the abusive family, of the corporation without conscience, of the system of injustice at work in courts and in the schools is the place of emergence, where the new old beings come up from the ground. These are precisely the sites where building can take place if we understand the resident stories, ghosts and mythical beings.

The next step for the builder in these foundation rites, after a place is chosen, is to mark off the site for building. What is it to be used for: domestic purposes, agriculture, religious practices? How large, what shape? To discover if the location is safe, four portions of bread, cheese and drink are placed in the corners where the building is to be constructed. If these are undisturbed, the omens are good for building.

Marking off the territory requires both a statement of claim and a show of strength; this foundation rite is also a form of throwing oneself on the mercy of the spirits of the place. One cannot defend the territory without their aid. If the spirits are not favorably inclined, a building will not stand, its story will not be good and it will not carry an inherent strength regardless of the materials chosen.

Marking off the territory one wants to claim is a bold statement: "this is the place I am choosing." A subtle understanding is also required, an understanding of the principles of energy available in the place. Where does the energy flow; where is the *chi?* Is the site guarded and protected, or open and vulnerable? Perhaps it is distinguished by a very particular story, such as the basilica of the Virgen de Guadalupe, who appeared to a peasant outside of Mexico City. Delimiting such a site is, of course, natural and supernatural, inspired by a divinity who does the marking. Perhaps there is a spring, a ray of light at dawn, a growth pattern of trees particularly beautiful, a well-angled hillside with a long view. Perhaps the site is mid-town in the visceral gut of the city.

In some traditions, the first marking is done by throwing a stone or hammer into the air while one's eyes are closed, setting the first corner where it lands. Marking a site really means simply "this is where I stand." We ask the question "where do you stand on this issue?" Where are you in this story?

For the father builder, the principle of claiming territory is to stand for his story, his family, his rule and his meaning—respecting and honoring the tradition of the place he is in and of those who have gone before him, and the spirits and stories of his fathers and grandfathers. Whether he has children or not, each man is a father inasmuch as he shelters and constructs the house of his experience for the children, wife, family and tribe that are within him at all times.

Once the site has been marked off, the third step for the builder is to lay the foundation. He must choose the materials and set a time for building. Timing, the design of the building, the laying out the perimeters of the foundation and physically putting the base in place are acts that hum with portent, with promise and with terror. In laying the foundation, one always attempts to avert evil, to draw luck, to find the best moment.

The essential act in laying the foundation is to placate and honor the old spirits and to call on new ones. Many times, before a new foundation may be constructed, an old building must be torn away or a place cleared and renewed. In laying the foundation, good workers are called—craftsmen, fellows; the contribution of the community is called upon.

What shall be built; how shall it be built and of what? The builder makes a place for himself, for his family and for his tribe. This is a place made in his heart as well as on the land.

In his book *A Pattern Language*, Christopher Alexander paints in detail the language of place as a mosaic of individual patterns—253 in his reckoning—which work together in every built place to create a coherent picture of a region: in its wider patterns—towns or country; in its patterns of neighborhood—local centers, transportation or movement, shopping areas, places of gathering, particular places for special groups of people (teenagers, children); and in the patterns developed and used in the construction of individual buildings. For example, one group of templates meant to describe possibilities for choices in buildings is as follows:

159. Light on two sides of every room
160. Building edge
161. Sunny place
162. North face

163. Outdoor room
164. Street windows
165. Opening to the street

Or, another grouping for minor rooms within the house:

179. Alcove
180. Window place
181 The fire
182. Eating atmosphere
183. Workspace enclosure
184. Cooking layout
185. Sitting circle
186. Communal sleeping
187. Marriage bed

(Pp. xxix–xxx)

Particular patterns thus father the foundation, providing the rules for establishing a made place. When the builder prepares his design and readies to lay the foundation, he finds in his heart these given patterns. Yahweh speaks in Exodus 25:8: "And let them make me a sanctuary that I may dwell among them, according to all that I show thee after the pattern of the tabernacle, and the pattern of all the instruments thereof." He continues by giving specific instructions for making a tabernacle. In I Chronicles 28:19, David speaks to his son Solomon of the design for building a house for God, "The Lord made me understand in writir.g by his hand upon me even all the works of this pattern."

The builder is spoken to by his father and grandfather, who give him the patterns for construction. In choosing materials for his building, he learns to find what is in their hearts. Solomon's temple was built of the oak, the date palm and the willow. Each tree has its spiritual power, a power to transform evil. Each tree has what the Japanese call *ramat*, "heart." For Odin, Yggdrassil (the World Ash) was the place of his knowledge of the mysteries of poetry and the runes. Buddha sat under the Bo Tree to gain understanding. The oak is sacred to Zeus and the cedar holds gifts for the shaman. For the Egyptians, the sky is a vast tree; we stand under its branches.

When the builder cuts a tree, he must follow specific rites. First, he makes a small cut. In this cavity, he puts food for the wood spirit, asking the spirit to depart so that he will not leave him homeless. Then he may chop down the tree.

The father builder seeks models of compassion. Compassion is what he builds, that is, a shelter for himself and others. When he builds, he is creating a temple. The word "temple" derives from *tempus*, "division"; he is setting a place apart, creating a challenge to time—*tempus*. And he is also attempting to create a temple to Eros by providing a gathering place for family and friends, a sanctuary, a place sanctified.

All the walls, gates and doors are thresholds he builds. These thresholds represent both the dividing and the joining of places. Each time he builds—whether he is making a structure or a friendship, a family, a career or a soul—he builds with the models of spirits, the models of the old stories, and he also attempts to call on new spirits.

He builds the labyrinth, a place of complexity, beauty, sacrifice of youth, forgetfulness, inflamed passions. He simultaneously erects the Tower of Babel. When a relationship starts, he builds toward heaven. He and his friend speak the same language. When the Tower is tall, they shoot arrows into the heavens; these come back bloody, and they know they have almost reached heaven. Then God confuses them; they no longer speak the same language. Chaos comes between them. They say, "We no longer communicate with each other." Chaos may give birth to Eros: "We stayed and talked and now we are closer together than ever before." So the Tower is begun again.

The builder makes an arena, a place for the collective where the spectacles happen; the community gathers for sports, competition, conflict and the boiling of blood. He builds a bridge—a place of peril, of transformation, of moving to the other side, joining the dark and light. It is said that God widens the bridge for the righteous and narrows it to the thickness of a hair for the unrighteous. The river below is fire, snakes, knives and blood. In the twelfth century in Europe, bridge-building brotherhoods were formed. These brotherhoods constructed chapels and hospitals by the sides of the bridges. This is the work of Eros, the work of connection. Since everyone must cross the bridges, this is the work of the family, of the "support group," of friendship.

The "men's group" is a craft guild, a bridge-building brotherhood, building the sanctuary, the kiva, the labyrinth, Babel. Men's groups are trying to re-craft the masculine out of materials more flexible and durable. They are creating an alloy honoring old spirits and calling new ones. They are forging a masculine of scrap metals. They are attempting to burn away both "machismo," a hard shell with a runny interior, and sentimentalism, a pudgy sweetness on the outside with a glacial brittle core. The metal of the new masculine seeks the consistency of the muscles of a general athlete. A good athlete's muscles, as opposed to those of a 'body builder,' are strong yet limber. He can feel pain and express it and also tolerate stress to the muscles. We do not know what the alloy will be like. The gathering and crafting of the new guilds of the masculine may help forge this new man made of old spirits honored and new spirits called.

The patriarch, one of the old spirits, is being honored, as are the bungler, the fool, the shaman and the warrior. Really, all spirits are as old as the heart of oak and older. The new ones called—aren't they the old ones gone for a time longer than memory, coming again out of the *shipapu*?

This guild of crafting among men is a building of a new patriarch, who honors the heart of the family as well as the heart of the masculine. He honors the tribe, the trees, the animals. Men's groups, the kiva group, are beginning to enter the sacred caves, the dark great pelvic interiors of the hidden ones, the grandmothers, the mothers, the lovers, the daughters. The discovery of the anima, the hidden cave within self, and her sisters, the women walking around, is a new and extraordinary mystery for the patriarch. Honoring the Goddess, the powers of the feminine, the dark unknown of feeling, the experience of helplessness, need, grief—these are the emergent beings coming up in the kiva for men, at the ground floor.

Our spiritual grandfathers told us that the time to lay the foundation was under a full moon—in the reflectiveness of night. Also, they told us to lay in the foundation a coin (symbol of the moon), herbs, bread and salt. In the foundation of the building should be nourishment, reflection, replenishment. Thus the father builder may return to the place of emergence, to reflection, to those qualities deep in the foundation which provide the sustaining of life.

Next in their foundation rites, the grandfathers showed us the model of the sacrifice. The Gods of the place demand that the building be laid up in blood. They demand the head of a person. The universal practice of sacrifice in the building has taken many forms. At times the builder himself has been sacrificed and walled into the structure, or his wife, or a young child, a virgin, a baker, a priest, a child sold by its mother. In later times, animals were sacrificed instead and walled in: fish, cats, dogs, doves, cattle, horses, goats.

What is really required is a life, and most specifically the head of a person. Building is a dangerous and all-consuming activity. Giving oneself over to a place—to claim a place, to lay one's foundation—is a sacrifice, a giving over of life. Little wonder that most people rent, have affairs or dream of "living elsewhere." Who wants to lose his head, to wall up his child or his favorite dog or the bird around him? Yet these are the things symbolically required of the father builder if he is to have *ramat,* heart.

Sorcerers, virgins, strangers, children, his own head, the animals (the instinctual side) he builds into the walls. He walls up his powers and his strengths. Standing under the oak, he lays up the foundation with bloody feet. A place heals and is healed to the extent it is held sacred by its occupant.

The house is guarded by Zeus Herkeios, divine protector. An image of Zeus Herkeios was found in every Greek home. This epithet, Herkeios, means "the whole family." Sometimes, Zeus is imaged as a snake, the protector of the grain bins. The snake is offered "panspermia," a mixture of water, oil and fruit, for protecting the storehouse.

Zeus was not the father of the Gods. He did not create man or the world. He is the paterfamilias, the head of the family. His name means "fence" or "barrier," the perimeter which contains the house, upholds the unwritten laws or customs and represents the moral order. Protecting the house requires getting down to the basics, down to the ground like the snake. A sacrifice of the higher things, of the "head," is required. Fixing the leaks, the malfunctions and the "problems" keeps the house "in good repair." The Zen master tells the young aspirant, "go wash the dishes." He does not say this to be clever or paradoxical; he means it literally. Building is dirty, bloody, tiring. The maintenance of a house, of a friendship, of a family takes dirty work, the sacrifice of the head.

A woman's son died. She went to the Buddha to ask him to restore her son to life. After much pleading, begging and crying on her part, the Buddha agreed, with a condition. The woman had to go house to house and discover one in which there had been no misfortune. She knocked on doors and heard the stories of the houses. Something new was born in her: she returned to the Buddha, telling him she realized that misfortune was universal and thanking him for the gift of compassion.

The body and the child are walled into the structures of whatever we build. The walls of tents are walls of movement, change, transformation, which honor the temporary, the uncertain, the inconstant. These are the tributes to Hermes and to Coyote. Those who move continuously through relationships, jobs and places honor Grandfather Coyote and have given up the heart of the founded oak; they have gone to live everywhere. Odysseus wandered the world of mysteries, but he longed to return home. The nomad endlessly seeks the Islands of the Blessed, the Seven Cities of Cibola, the Palace of Circe and attempts to make a heart created of change and uncertainty. He buries his head in the sky, which is a different type of foundation.

The final step in the foundation rites given by the ancestral grandfathers is celebration and incubation. The first being to cross the threshold of the new place will die first. Transformation, entering into new dimensions, exacts a toll. One might send a dog or cat across the threshold of the new building, but the father builder may just as well pass this space himself, since the day and hour of death are marked in the book of God.

In ancient Greece, when one desired understanding of the will of the God, he could practice incubation, that is, going to sleep in the God's temple to dream and observing the dreams the next day. Incubation, that is, attention to the emergence and speaking of the God, is a process of great importance in the building of houses, of friendships and of families. What our lover says to us in the dream may be the foundation of what she says to us in the daytime.

The celebration of the crossing of the threshold is the celebration of entering the center of creation and the center of the labyrinth. This is the place where old spirits are to be honored and new spirits called. Each dinner celebrated is the Eucharist, the sacrifice, the feast, celebrated according to the story of psyche told in the family and the tribe. The house is the Garden of Eden, Erewhon, Atlantis, the center of the labyrinth, *The 1001 Arabian Nights,* the beautiful spring where Coyote sees the lovely girl, Poseidon's angry seas.

The Philosopher's Body

The philosopher's body is a tissue made entirely of oppositions. Driven by indulgence, he reins himself with deprivation; entirely informed by the sensual, he nonetheless professes his devotion to abstraction; though his belly is full of conceptions, he pays homage to heady perception; though his amour is death, he holds vigil all night long and never sleeps; though oblivion calls him, hankering is stronger; though his element is water, his prose is brittle and lacks all humidity. He is torn forever between the left and right testicle, female and male. He suffers from *mentula loquens* and yet sits quiet the whole day; yet if he speaks, he utters not a word but a river of testament. What he grasps he disbelieves, and what he disbelieves he cannot grasp; when he sits under the Bo tree, he assumes he has found wisdom and forgets that he has found a tree.

The Philosopher's Pater

As the philosopher sits under the Bo tree, feigning his disinterest in the three beautiful daughters of Lord Kama—Desire, Fulfillment and Regret—he glows in his enlightenment. Perhaps, however, soon he is approached by a hunter who asks him, who is your father? And, where is your wound? And, why are you under the tree when the body of man lives in the tree?

So perhaps it is because the Buddha is sitting on the ground beneath the Bo tree that he has become enraptured. Perhaps he is smiling not because his head has ruled and reined in the unruly body after all, but because his testicles and loins—the Buddha is not a *castrado*—are touching the warm ground below his robe. His secret sensuality—we know of his life before his Great Going Forth—is so absolutely potent that what he needed was not the overwhelming flesh of the Palace for his rapture but the mere touch of clay on his subtle epidermis. The philosopher's knowing—often concealed in the interpretation of those quite outside the *vital circle* of his body—is simple. He knows that there is *hankering* and that there is *oblivion* and that the body is the sole and final testament to these.

The mind, however, rebukes simplicity and loves the complex; St. Paul, a man driven by concerns about sexuality but led by the fashion of the mind prevailing in his milieu, was thrown into the mind's madness when he discovered the simplicity of hankering and oblivion and, thus, set out with all his might to scorn and refuse what his phallus told him and to lay down the hunter's body and the builder's body and create a *symbolism of the tree of Christ.* He believed that mystery and hiddenness and disbelief (he called them *faith*) would quiet the genitals, the hand, the eye, the legs. And did he not run thousands of miles preaching, receiving the pounding of stones on his body in a physical ecstasy?

Let us recall the great sensualist René Descartes, as he sits by his fireplace purportedly attempting to "discover if anything exists." This passage is from his "Second Meditation," subtitled "Of the Nature of the Human Mind, and That It Is More Easily Known Than the Body" (*Discourse on Method and Meditations,* pp. 86–88):

> Let us now consider the commonest things, which are commonly believed to be the most distinctly known and the easiest of all to know, namely, the bodies which we touch and see. I do not intend to speak of bodies in general, for general notions are usually somewhat more confused; let me rather consider one body in particular. Let us take, for example, this bit of wax which has just been taken from the hive. It has not yet completely lost the sweetness of the honey it contained; it still retains something of the odor of the flowers from which it was collected; its color, shape, and size are apparent; it is hard and cold; it can easily be touched, and, if you knock on it, it will give out some sound. Thus, everything which can make a body distinctly known is found in this example.
>
> But now while I am talking, I bring it close to the fire. What remains of the taste evaporates; the odor vanishes; its color changes; its shape is lost; its size increases; it becomes liquid; it grows hot; one can hardly touch it; and although it is knocked upon, it will give out no sound. Does the same wax remain after this change? We must admit that it does; no one denies it, no one judges otherwise. What is it then in this bit of wax that we recognize with so much distinctness? Certainly it cannot be anything that I observed by means of the senses, since everything in the field of taste, smell, sight, touch, and hearing is changed, and since the same wax nevertheless remains.

> The truth of the matter perhaps, as I now suspect, is that this was neither that sweetness of honey, nor that pleasant odor of flowers, nor that whiteness, nor that shape, nor that sound, but only a body which a little while ago appeared to my senses under these forms, and which now makes itself felt under others, but what is it to speak precisely, that I imagine when I conceive it in this fashion? Let us consider it attentively and, rejecting everything that does not belong to the wax, see what remains. Certainly nothing is left but something extended, flexible, and movable. But what is meant by flexible and movable? Does it consist of becoming square and of passing from the square into a triangular shape? Certainly not . . .

Descartes proceeds from this and other examples to attempt to prove that we find no consistently adequate definition satisfying to the mind that allows us to call the body the body—that only thinking maintains that "certain" pervasive sameness to allow us to call it "real." May not one see the same tissue of opposition and rebuking of simple hankering and oblivion in Descartes as in St. Paul?

Descartes gives himself away, revealing his body of flesh in the passage quoted. The vividness of imagery of the wax— its color, texture, odor (which change with fire, thus proving that they are of the same body as the philosopher)— does not escape us. The hankering of Descartes—his lust for the touch of hand, for eye, belly, the builder's body (the body of the potter)—lurks translucently lit by the warm firelight. Whatever abstractions or arguments or conceptions he bears through the rest of the many pages of the "Meditations" carry unmistakably the sweet scent of honey, the lingering embrace of the wax on the fingers—especially when the hot wax burns the fingers with its liquidity; what is inescapable from the "Meditations" is the corporeality of the world, the presence of the philosopher's body which explores wax and fire in sensual proximity. Far from escaping, through elegant argument, the body (and though he attempts through intellection to return the body to existence later in the "Meditations," the argument falls flaccid), Descartes demonstrates the presence of his body, the hankering after sensual experience, and immerses us into the immediacy of his pleasure.

Descartes attempts to demonstrate that the body cannot be proved to exist. Oddly enough, he creates a finally eloquent demonstration of the endurance and continuity of physical existence, of the body and of sensate experience. That change and movement and flux and complex identity exist in the body is shown in his example. Volatility is one of the most fundamental characteristics of matter, perhaps its only "security." How we identify matter is that it transmutes.

Lust and Water

Because lust is strongest in the philosopher, he must abstain or lose the richness of sensual experience he knows is the father of his thought. What he would do if untethered is restrained by the philosopher not—as the religious have interpreted in their sloggard fear and dullness—because of moral hatred of the body (though some have written so, fearing extinction by the deadly Churches of history), but because he knows that the full experience of the body comes only through patience, time and developed taste.

The extraction of pleasure in bodily experience is a

complex matter requiring years of practice, skill and sensitivity. Though the father rarely has the opportunity to tutor his son in amorous instruction, blessed is the philosopher who gains a pupil he can chastely educate in the fine art of Aphrodite. The philosopher father's *work* is tolerance, understanding and the conveying of any knowledge he may be able to give regarding the life of the body and the mind.

Among the Plains Indians exists the image of *mentula loquens*, or the "talking privates." In many stories, the phallus advises man of what he desires to know. On some occasions, the phallus is known to escape for a while for adventures on his own; in such cases, the philosopher's body remains— we may assume—rather decreased in lust, but also diminished in loquaciousness, motivation and desire for self-reflection and self-knowing. One may suspect many recent philosophers of having banished all parts of their bodies from speech, thus depriving philosophy of its father, the body, as well as of the house, the tree, clay and any filling of the belly.

The Adam's apple, that symbol of undigested carnal experience, serves poorly as a scrotum, being far too high in the body, too close to the arrogant brain, too closely aligned with the choke response. Being too early in the digestive process to appreciate the many functions and pleasures of the body, it easily aligns itself with something we call consciousness. Adam, whose name means "clay," could well digest earth. He was made from four types of clay; his body reached from earth to heaven and was of extreme beauty and brightness. God made his bones from rocks, his eyes from the light of the sun, his hair from grass, his blood from water, his spirit from the clouds. It took a millennium for his soul to enter his body. When it entered and he found the ecstasy of physical existence, he was as loathe to leave as he was to enter. When he was cast from the Garden, he quickly grabbed up tools—hammers, tongs and a needle—with which to build the world. The apple which stuck in his throat was compounded of good and evil, a complex fruit. To eat of this fruit was an act of courage, a challenge of his God on the God's own turf, the philosopher's courage. Ever since Adam, men have meditated by trees, repeating the courageous act of questioning divinity.

What Adam could not swallow—nor can any man, nor should any man—was leaving a Garden, his body, wherein all lust was requited. The country of that Garden—country here being taken again in its sense of "land lying in opposites"—is marked by the gate out into the land of oppositionalism. What is different in this land is not duality, because that existed in the Garden between man and God, already foreshadowing the wild search for dualisms to follow for the eons, but rather a poly-ality, where oppositionalisms of all sorts would blossom in every quarter. If we see psychology as the knowing of psyche or soul, we see that the soul of man since Adam is riddled everywhere with opposites. Remember that the body is a *concreteness,* a growing together of parts, all of which have their own lives and their own births, all of which compete and strive for full presence and power.

Having been driven from the Garden, the philosopher enters the desert and hankers forever for the humid temperateness of the natural body. Though he lives in arid abstraction, his beloved element is water, the primal fluids. Whereas the hunter requires countrysides to roam in pursuit of encounters with the fleeing body and the builder needs a meeting of fields, trees and stones to practice his arts of separation and unification, the philosopher's body requires water. The philosopher burns and thirsts unceasingly and forever seeks the *refrigerium*—a Near East symbol for the cooling draught which refreshes and restores vitality and passion. Dahlberg writes, "The sole labor of the water mind is to find out what is primal" (p. 42). The philosopher seeks forever what is primal, that is, the body, which is symbolized for him by water: the river is time; the ocean is infinity. The coursing of blood, which brings lust to every appendage of the philosopher's body, is examined and reexamined in its labyrinthine path by the philosopher for the discovery of the source and meaning of his lust—referred to by Bergson as *élan vital* and by Schopenhauer as *will*—yet the primal font is never located, unless it be the heart, an organ reviled by philosophers as untrustworthy and unintelligent.

Buddha tells Sariputra in *The Heart Sutra,* "Oh, Sariputra, it is because of his non-attainment that a Boddhisattva, through having relied on the perfection of wisdom alone, dwells without thought coverings." The ridding of "thought-coverings" purportedly achieved by meditation is achieved rather by Buddha sitting in the Garden under the Bo tree with his testicles and loins touching the clay woman-body, that is, the hot soil which he knows to be paradise. This is the wisdom he is referring to, the coursing of blood, the philosopher's inner river, through belly, Adam's apple, arms, legs, scrotum and loins.

When Descartes's ball of wax was finally transformed by heat to warm liquid, barely able to be touched, he saw that he had attempted to grasp the infinite ocean. Always punctual, Kant, walking through Königsberg, checks his watch against the town clock, to assure himself that the river is still running down to the sea. Victor Hugo, referred to by his contemporaries as the "*homme océan*," produces work in every area of human culture in order to follow the ineluctable coursing of the blood in every particle of the body. Alan Watts writes of Zen and seeks fulfillment in sensual pleasure in his house by the sea and on his boat. Jorge Manrique writes in his "Coplas a la muerte de su padre" ("Lines for His Father's Death")

> Nuestras vidas son los ríos
> que van a dar en la mar

("our lives are rivers/moving to the sea"), thus freely acknowledging—with that characteristic depth and directness of the Spaniard—the relationship of water, the mind, the philosopher's body and his inevitable connection with his father. Gaston Bachelard writes of suffering, speech, stones, memory and time in this passage from his search for the primal and its relationship with water:

> Come, oh my friends, on a clear morning to sing the stream's vowels! Where is our first suffering? We have hesitated to say. . . . It was born in the hours when we have hoarded within us things left unsaid. Even so, the stream will teach you to speak; in spite of the pain and the memories, it will teach you euphoria through euphemism, energy through poems. Not a moment will pass without repeating some lovely round word that rolls over the stones. (P. 195)

The powerful forces which surge in the philosopher's body may be likened to a dark night river which threatens to destroy all which it encounters. The "water's dark body" carries the quality of indulgence, harm and suffering which St. Paul so feared in the rising of priapic energies; St. Paul feared that what would wash to the sea, to the infinite, would be the trash of the town, the debris of bodily experience, polluting the heavenly ocean. Thus the seminal fluids of man must suffer restraining, though he burn and travail.

Yet as the philosopher knows, what separates divides, and the waters that harm are those that heal as well. When he extends his body, embracing the arms, belly, legs, moving to encounter the "other," only the fluid interchange with that other may offer the occasion of the entire experience of that other. The region where such signification, structure and movement are prepared—that is, belly, arms, legs, hands, mouth, what is extended by the philosopher in his encounter with the other—is that region joined by the coursing of waters which the philosopher knows to be primal, remembering himself as Adam and the body as the humid Garden through which courses his hankering.

In his awareness of oppositions, the philosopher senses both the still, uniting waters, the waters of Lethe, oblivion, drunk by the souls who are to be reborn, so that they might forget the harm of their former lives, and the turbid, muscular Yellowstone River in Montana thrusting through the deep canyons, seminally sparking a hundred billion acres of garden on its hejira to the ocean.

All joining with the other—other bodies, psyches, with stone, tree, clay or the beloved—is hankering and oblivion. The philosopher can neither fully spiritualize the body nor fully incorporate the spirit, if indeed such a thing as spirit exists outside of the coursing of water.

Sexual Battle

The philosopher's body, a tissue fed with and made entirely of oppositions, discovers fulfillment, completion and complement—that is to say, strife and opposition—in the body and being of woman.

Aristotle, Thomas Aquinas and Freud all referred to woman as "mutilated man"; the word "mutilated" comes from Latin *mutilus,* which originally meant "short." Plato held that the human being was originally a sphere which has been split, and the two parts—male and female—have sought each other for completion ever since.

The philosopher, whose calling it is to find the lost Garden, the body, seeks in his tissue of opposition that being with whom he can encounter opposition and completeness. This "single form" comes into being through the uniting of opposites; a uniting of sames by joining two bases and feet would not create a vessel but an aberration, a monster. A vessel has a foot, a base—and a belly, shoulder and lip.

Zeus and Hera quarrel without cease, not as a moral lesson for mortals, but as a *tat twam asi*—"thou art that"—a description, a mirror to men and women of their opposition. Hera was purportedly under the domination of Zeus and in obeisance to him, but she refused his power on many occasions through her stubbornness, her own need for opposition and the need she knew her husband's body felt. Zeus attempted beating her, with ill result and no greater obedience: psyche and water are unmoved by threat. He chained her and suspended her in the clouds to force submission, knowing alas, as St. Paul did, that forced submission of the body creates foul dreams.

Hera grew more subtle and inflamed Zeus's passion by wearing the girdle of Aphrodite; the philosopher boils for touch, hankers for union no more than the Gods nor any less. Jealous by nature, habit and through curiosity, Hera punished her husband, who expected no less; when his interest rose, hers flagged. He became parched, but his mind filled with water and primal encounter; she remained moist but out of reach. "A dry head in a man," as Heraclitus testifies, "is the best, but a moist body which sucks up the dew of the rainy Hyades is the wisest in a woman" (Dahlberg, p. 28). Zeus, knowing this, attempted argument, that mock and deluding model of the war of opposites which resolves nothing and leaves the body drained and sad. He quarreled with her about which sex was more capable of gratification in bed; they called in the hermaphrodite Tiresias. Tiresias, who lacked the philosopher's hankering, answered what everyone knows: "Woman." Hera struck him blind, a redundancy, since he already was incapable of seeing the suffering in the body of Zeus and of taking pity on him. The philosopher requires opposition, and Tiresias in his blindness offered resolution. In an act sometimes read as compassion, Zeus bestowed that cruelest ability of all on him, the talent which takes away all passion and oppositions, the power to see and know the future. This assured his empty androgyny.

Nietzsche writes:

> The qualities in women which inspire respect—or fear—are her greatest naturalness, her flexibility and craft, her tigress claw, her naivete, her uneducability, her instinctive cruelty, her immense passions and virtues. In spite of this fear, she excites pity by appearing

more afflicted, more fragile, more necessitous of love,
and more liable to disillusions than any other creature.
Man has been arrested before women with one foot
already in tragedy! Is woman about to be disenchanted?
(Mencken, p. 23)

The philosopher, who lacks flexibility and craft but lives
rather on his scrotum, will desire union with woman's being more than his own life.

Jung writes that

> Although man and woman unite they nevertheless
> represent irreconcilable opposites which, when acti-
> vated, degenerate into deadly hostility. This primordial
> pair of opposites symbolizes every conceivable pair of
> opposites that may occur: hot and cold, light and dark,
> north and south, dry and damp, good and bad, con-
> scious and unconscious. (*CW* 12, ¶192).

How quickly he moves to abstraction, the great oblivion, to
escape his fear of concreteness, of speaking of the struggle
of the hostile and longed-for hankering of the prepuce.

Jung reminds us of the passion of Adam:

> Although enmity was put only between the serpent and
> the woman (Genesis 3:15), this curse nevertheless fell
> upon the relationship of the sexes in general. Eve was
> told: "Thy desire shall be to thy husband, and he shall
> rule over thee." And Adam was told: "Cursed is the
> ground for thy sake . . . because thou hast hearkened
> unto the voice of thy wife" (3:16f.). Primal guilt lies be-

tween them, an *interrupted state of enmity,* and this appears unreasonable only to our rational mind but not to our psychic nature. (*CW* 14, ¶104)

Now we remember why Buddha smiled under the Bo tree, since he once again touched the good woman's clay with loins and testicles.

Jung reminds us of the primal oppositionalism in the philosopher's body again; but we see that he is a man with the concomitant fear of the "immense passions and virtues" of the body of woman and the suffering in the body of man. He falls into the temptation of St. Paul; he *spiritualizes*:

> Our reason is often influenced far too much by purely physical considerations, so that the union of the sexes seems to it the only sensible thing and the urge for union the most sensible instinct of all. But if we conceive of nature in the higher sense as the totality of all phenomena, then the physical is only one of her aspects, the other is pneumatic or spiritual. . . . Because it overvalues the physical, our contemporary reason lacks spiritual orientation, that is, pneuma. (*CW* 14, ¶104)

Might one say, rather, that our contemporary reason utterly ignores the philosopher's body—as well as the hunter's and the builder's?

Yet Adam needs his oblivion as well as his hankering; we cannot blame the philosopher who recoils for an instant before the body of woman and his own body any more than we can the hunter who hesitates and suffers momentarily before the death of the enchanting animal. "Jesus hides his genitals with a napkin or by his hand" (Dahlberg, p. 19), and so we know that he truly wore the body of Adam and of the philosopher, that he burned with hankering like other men.

The Philosopher in His Village

The philosopher offers his body to the community, to his family and to his own fulfillment. His hand grasps the knife, which he may use for defense, for cutting meat or for the display of power. His legs move in dance and lead him in his voice, with which he sings. He fills his belly with the flesh killed by his hunter's body.

"Protection" (from Latin *pro-tegere*, to "offer covering") he presents by offering his extended body, the body of the builder, to cover against insults or invasion. Hospitality, a word connected with host and ghost, is what he offers of his meat and wine, the fruit of his own doing, to guests. He satisfies their hankering while expressing his interest in oblivion—his own invisibility.

Where the coursing of his own blood through belly, scrotum, legs, arms, Adam's apple, phallus, hands and eyes has grown still and his body and the body of woman no longer seek enmity and union, where he has lost the connection with his suffering and male sexuality, the philosopher's body is dust, and less than dust.

Return to Father

To reclaim the patriarch and the masculine is to reclaim the world, to re-enter and live anew the vibrant, pulsating, fighting, rolling, consumptive world.

Return to father means a return home, a *repair*—to our images, to our language and to our ancient home in the psyche, in the body and in the natural world.

Return to father means reclaiming responsiveness; ending harm to the natural world; living as fathers again; honoring craftsmanship; building well; being honest.

Return to father means reclaiming the patriarch in all his forms—as warrior, father, hunter, builder, philosopher. It means a return home to honoring the earth where we live, a return home to mountain, river, field, panther, dream.

Port Townsend, Washington 1986
Last Chance, Idaho 1987
Kansas City, Missouri 1988

Works Cited

Alexander, Christopher. *A Pattern Language.* New York: Oxford University Press, 1977.

———. *The Timeless Way of Building.* New York: Oxford University Press, 1979.

Bachelard, Gaston. *Water and Dreams: An Essay on the Imagination of Matter.* Translated by Edith R. Farrell. Dallas: Pegasus Foundation, 1983.

Barnstone, Willis. *Borges at Eighty.* Bloomington: Indiana University Press, 1982.

Berry, Wendell. *Collected Poems.* San Francisco: North Point Press, 1985.

Bly, Robert. *The Man in the Black Coat Turns.* New York: Dial, 1981.

Campbell, Joseph. *The Inner Reaches of Outer Space: Metaphor as Myth and as Religion.* New York: Alfred Van Der Marck, 1986.

Dahlberg, Edward. *Can These Bones Live?* New York: New Directions, 1965.

Descartes, René. *Discourse on Method and Meditations.* Indianapolis: Bobbs-Merrill, 1960.

Eliade, Mircea. *Rites and Symbols of Initiation: The Mysteries of Birth and Rebirth.* New York: Harper & Row, 1958.

Ficino, Marsilio. *The Book of Life.* Translated by Charles Boer. Dallas: Spring Publications, 1980.

Firestone, Ross, ed. *A Book of Men: Visions of the Male Experience.* New York: Stonehill, 1978.

Fowles. *The Tree.* Boston: Little Brown, 1979.

Gurdjieff, G. I. *Meetings with Remarkable Men.* New York: E. P. Dutton, 1974.

Heidegger, Martin. *Being and Time.* Translated by John Macquarrie and Edward Robinson. New York: Harper & Row, 1962.

Hillman, James. *Inter Views: Conversations with Laura Pozzo on Psychotherapy, Biography, Love, Soul, Dreams, Work, Imagination, and the State of the Culture.* New York: Harper & Row, 1983. (Reprinted Dallas: Spring Publications, 1991)

———. *The Myth of Analysis: Three Essays in Archetypal Psychology.* New York: Harper & Row, 1972.

———. "Senex and Puer." In *Puer Papers.* Edited by James Hillman. Dallas: Spring Publications, 1979.

———. *The Thought of the Heart.* Dallas: Spring Publications, 1981.

James, William. "Does 'Consciousness' Exist?" In *Essays in Radical Empiricism* (1912). Cambridge: Harvard University Press, 1976.

Jung, C. G. *The Collected Works of C. G. Jung.* Translated by R. F. C. Hull. Bollingen Series XX. Princeton: Princeton University Press:

Vol. 9 Part I, *The Archetypes and the Collective Unconscious,* 1959.

Vol. 12 *Psychology and Alchemy,* 1953.

Vol. 14 *Mysterium Coniunctionis,* 1965.

———. *Memories, Dreams, Reflections.* Recorded and edited by Aniela Jaffé. New York: Vintage Books, 1961.

Klein, Ernest. *A Comprehensive Etymological Dictionary of the English Language: Dealing with the Origin of Words and Their Sense Development, Thus Illustrating the History of Civilization and Culture.* New York: Elsevier, 1971.

Leach, Maria and Jerome Fried, eds. *Funk and Wagnall's Standard*

Dictionary of Folklore, Mythology and Legend. New York: Harper & Row, 1984.

Lerner, Gerda. *The Creation of Patriarchy.* New York: Oxford University Press, 1986.

Lockhart, Russell A. *Words as Eggs: Psyche in Language and Clinic.* Dallas: Spring Publications, 1983.

MacDiarmid, Hugh. *The Complete Poems of Hugh MacDiarmid.* Edited by Michael Grieve and W. R. Aitken. 2 vols. New York: Penguin, 1985.

Mencken, Henry L. *The Gist of Nietzsche.* Boston: John W. Luce, 1910.

Michaelis, David. *The Best of Friends.* New York: William Morrow & Co., 1983.

Ortega y Gasset, José. *Meditations on Hunting.* Translated by Howard B. Wescott. New York: Charles Scribner's Sons, 1972.

Rawson, Philip. *Ceramics.* Philadelphia: University of Pennsylvania Press, 1984.

———. "On Being There." *Studio Potter* 13/2 (1985).

Schneiders, Sandra. *Women and the Word: The Gender of God in the New Testament and the Spirituality of Women.* Mahwah, N.J.: Paulist Press, 1986.

Snyder, Gary. *Axe Handles.* San Francisco: North Point Press, 1983.

Thass-Thienemann, Theodore. *The Interpretation of Language.* 2 vols. New York: Aronson, 1973.

Thompson, Keith. "What Men Really Want: A *New Age* Interview with Robert Bly." *New Age,* May 1982.

Webster's New World Dictionary of the English Language. New York: World Publishing Co., 1968.

Related Readings

Aristotle. *The Nichomachean Ethics.* Translated by H. Rackham. Cambridge: Harvard University Press, 1982.

Benthall, Jonathan and Ted Polhemus, eds. *The Body as a Medium of Expression.* New York: E. P. Dutton, 1975.

Biemel, Walter. *Martin Heidegger: An Illustrated Study.* New York: Harcourt Brace Jovanovich, 1976.

Budge, E. A. Wallis. *The Gods of the Egyptians: Or Studies in Egyptian Mythology.* Vol. 2. New York: Dover, 1969.

Campbell, Joseph. *The Masks of God.* 4 vols.: *Occidental Mythology, Oriental Mythology, Primitive Mythology, Creative Mythology.* New York: Viking.

———. *The Mythic Image.* Princeton: Princeton University Press, 1974.

Canetti, Elias. *Crowds and Power.* New York: Farrar, Straus, and Giroux, 1984.

———. *Earwitness: Fifty Characters.* New York: Farrar, Straus, and Giroux, 1979.

Carlyon, Richard. *A Guide to the Gods.* New York: Quill, 1982.

Clarkston, Atelia and Gilbert C. Cross, eds. *World Folktales: A Scribner Resource Collection.* New York: Charles Scribner's Sons, 1980.

Dahlberg, Edward. *The Confessions of Edward Dahlberg.* New York: George Braziller, 1971.

Eliade, Mircea. *The Sacred and the Profane: The Nature of Religion.* New York: Harcourt Brace Jovanovich, 1959.

Graves, Robert. *The White Goddess: A Historical Grammar of Poetic Myth.* New York: Farrar, Straus, and Giroux, 1984.

Hillman, James. *Re-Visioning Psychology.* New York: Harper & Row, 1975.

———. "Wars, Arms, Rams, Mars: On the Love of War." In *Facing Apocalypse.* Dallas: Spring Publications, 1987.

Jung, C. G. *C. G. Jung Speaking: Interviews and Encounters.* Edited by William McGuire and R. F. C. Hull. Princeton: Princeton University Press, 1977.

———. *The Collected Works of C. G. Jung.* Translated by R. F. C. Hull. Bollingen Series XX. Princeton: Princeton University Press; especially the following:

Vol. 5 *Symbols of Transformation,* 1956.

Vol. 8 *The Structure and Dynamics of the Psyche,* 1960.

Vol. 16 *The Practice of Psychotherapy,* 1954.

Vol. 17 *The Development of Personality,* 1954.

———. *Seminar Notes on Psychological Analysis of Nietzsche's Zarathustra.* Compiled by Mary Briner in ten volumes. Zürich, 1942.

Kalven, Janet and Mary I. Buckley. *Women's Spirit Bonding.* New York: Pilgrim, 1984.

Kerényi, Carl. *The Gods of the Greeks.* London: Thames and Hudson, 1950.

———. *The Heroes of the Greeks.* London: Thames and Hudson, 1959.

Leonard, George. "The Warrior." *Esquire,* July 1986, pp. 64–71.

Lévi-Strauss, Claude. *The Savage Mind.* Chicago: University of Chicago Press, 1966.

Miller, Casey and Kate Swift. *Words and Women.* Garden City, New York: Doubleday, 1977.

Morris, Desmond. *Manwatching: A Field Guide to Human Behavior.* New York: Harry N. Abrams, 1977.

Sun Tzu. *The Art of War.* Foreword by James Clavell. New York: Delacorte Press, 1983.

Wulff, Lee. *Trout on a Fly.* New York: Nick Lyons Books, 1986.

Related Readings

Oedipus Variations
Karl Kerényi, James Hillman
In this book the famous mythographer Karl Kerényi widens the cultural context of the Oedipus myth by commenting incisively on versions of the drama played in Rome, Paris, Vienna, and London. James Hillman takes on Father Freud, inverting the emphasis of the Oedipus complex: why do fathers kill their sons? Hillman also looks at the anima landscape of Colonus where old Oedipus, helped by his daughters, dies. He further shows that, in addition to the curse, murder, incest, and disease, the myth contained beauty, blessing, love, and loyalty. (170 pp.)

Fathers and Mothers
Bly, Hillman, Vitale et al.
Twelve chapters break old habits of thinking about family. Robert Bly and James Hillman on the agonies of father–son love; Ursula K. Le Guin's Persephonic prose poem; Marion Woodman on changes in the mother image during analysis; the stepmother; the mothering of desire. The classic essay by Erich Neumann on matriarchal moon consciousness and C. G. Jung's original 1938 "The Mother Archetype." (259 pp.)

Broodmales
Nor Hall, Warren R. Dawson
Men becoming women? In the folk customs of couvade, a man takes on the events of a woman's body—pregnancy, labor, nursing—so that her experience becomes his. Rather bizarre than perverse or deluded, these behaviors reveal a natural symbolic process, which Hall's essay explains psychologically. Dawson's classic crosscultural study gathers evidence for what often still occurs today in men's private experiences. (173 pp.)

Spring Publications, Inc.   P.O. Box 222069   Dallas, Texas 75222